T0038998

AFTER THE FACT

AFTER THE FACT

Volume 2

If & When

Volume 3

Here & Now

Marvin Bell and Christopher Merrill

WHITE PINE PRESS ❖ BUFFALO, NEW YORK

White Pine Press
P.O. Box 236
Buffalo, NY 14201
www.whitepine.org

Copyright © 2023 by Christopher Merrill & the estate of Marvin Bell

All rights reserved. This work, or portions thereof, may not be reproduced in any form
without the written permission of the publisher.

Publication of this book was supported by public funds from the New York State Council
on the Arts, with the support of Governor Kathy Hochul and the New York State Legis-
lature, a State Agency, and with generous support from the University of Iowa's Office of
the Vice President and College of Liberal Arts and Sciences.

Acknowledgements:
        If & When
                #1-60 *The Georgia Review*
                #25 and #55 *Stone Gathering*
                #61-68 *december*
                #70-73 *The Fiddlehead*
                #74-77 82-90 *Air/Light*

        Here & Now
                #1-4 *Air/Light*
                #19-24 *AGNI*

Cover Image: marukopum

Printed and bound in the United States of America.

ISBN 978-1-945680-72-4

Library of Congress Control Number: 2022950766

Table of Contents

When

Volume III
Here & Now

Here

Now

Preface

After the Fact: If & When is a sequel to the 2016 book *After the Fact: Scripts & Postscripts*, ninety linked paragraphs written in 2011-2015 with Christopher Merrill, whom I first met in 1978. It was Chris' idea to start a back-and-forth collaboration. By turns it has felt like prose poetry, lyrical nonfiction, poetic memoir, and emotive journalism. It is a conversation in which we take up matters biographical, philosophical, sociopolitical, and aesthetic. Neither of us realized at the start how much it would come to mean to us. Hence, *If & When* following *After the Fact*. Because Chris undertakes cultural diplomacy missions for the State Department, his paragraphs arrive from all over the world, while mine have been sent from Iowa City, Iowa, and Port Townsend, Washington.

We have included in this volume four paragraphs written on the occasion of editor Stephen Corey's retirement August 1, 2019, after thirty-six years with *The Georgia Review*. The first sixty of these paragraphs first appeared in *The Georgia Review*, as had thirty from *After the Fact*. No. 89 in this series is titled "Aesthetic Wobble #6" because the first five aesthetic wobbles appeared in *After the Fact: Scripts & Postscripts*.

—M.B.

Marvin and I completed the second volume of *After the Fact*, subtitled *If & When*, in the early days of the pandemic, and while we could not imagine how long the initial lockdown would last or what toll it might take on our lives, we knew the novel coronavirus would not only change the nature of our collaboration, which had heretofore depended to a certain degree upon the tension between what I experienced during my international travels and what Marvin was thinking about closer to home, but also force us to document and reflect on the sudden changes thrust upon us. Thus began *Here & Now*, the projected third volume of *After the Fact*, which we imagined would consist of ninety entries, as in the two preceding volumes. But Marvin's death on December 14, 2020 brought an end to our collaboration, and so this book concludes with my twenty-ninth entry. The blank space on the last page is larger than I thought possible.

—C.M.

Volume II

If & When

If

MB:
Dead Fish

Roger points out that, in writing about a certain cornet solo, I have used the word "counterpoint" where the better term is "obbligato." Alas, it seems the term "obbligato" has lost the firm cast of the obligatory to the flaccid tinge of the optional, from necessity to superfluous. I return in the past to the Monday Night Band. A lawyer sitting first chair cornet, a congressman on the timpani, I was the one grade-schooler allowed, assigned to play the third cornet parts. It was "Tubby the Tuba" time, a divertissement for a summer concert, and this rehearsal night suddenly there was another squirt on third cornet. Even in "Tubby," this pipsqueak, with his odd embouchure, was re-markable. And he was smoking a cigar!—flicking the ash into a straight mute. By such circuitous paths as limn the otherwise circumscribed lives of small towns, we would meet up years later, bestowing on first cornet scores such subversive grace notes and high Cs as might be allowed. More resonant still are the times we lingered in the car, laughing uncontrollably inside con-versations about ideas. Quite a card, that Camus. What a jokester, Sartre. Pulling the rug out from under big ideas, like embellishing the music, was our way to be in the game. Philosophers had been thrown in the hoosegow for their words. The town creek stunk from dead fish. Whatever we thought, we knew not to let on.

CM:
Storytelling

Obliged to write for an undersecretary of state a paragraph on the importance of storytelling, I thought of Scheherazade, the vizier's daughter, who enchanted a murderous king for one thousand and one nights, prolonging her life until he fell in love with her and made her queen. Easy to forget how she prepared for this campaign, reading books on history, art, and philosophy, memorizing poems, learning her craft—which she deployed in the service of suspense, weaving together tales from different traditions, many of them set in Baghdad. I brought the abridged version of the tales on my first visit to the city, and during a security briefing at the embassy, which included instructions for injecting vaccines in the event of a chemical attack, I recalled the story of an old fisherman breaking the seal of Solomon on a copper jar hauled up in his net and releasing a *djinn*, who has resolved to kill his liberator. The fisherman tricks the *djinn* back into the jar, then tells him a story about compassion, refusing to free him again until he promises not to hurt him—which the *djinn* does, generating more stories. It was too late to secure such a promise from the Iraqi insurgents, whose skill in setting off suicide car bombs governed my trips out of the Green Zone; hence the diplomatic community had concluded that a new storyline must be devised for the broken country. One night at dinner a public affairs officer asked for titles of books on the art of writing fiction. Inspired by Scheherazade's lifelong literary apprenticeship, I said, "Once upon a time, in the city of Baghdad..."

MB:
The Town of None of Your Business

My childhood friend Peter mixes us a special Brazilian drink. His law firm does a lot of work in Brazil, and he speaks Portuguese which, along with an Ivy League degree, would make him an outsider in our hometown. Unlike me, he never tried to pass. His daffy nerviness brought him rewards, and his German mother greeted him each day after school as if they were reconnecting after a long separation. *Liebchen! Liebchen!* she cried out as she rushed to embrace him. Every school day, *Liebchen! Liebchen!* as I stood by. A mother most unusual for the time, thought "peculiar," who made pottery, wrote a journal, played the violin, and served as my second mother when I needed one. None of your business why. That's where I come from, the town of "None of Your Business." Peter's father, the physicist, says little, each day returns from the labs and hurries into his study to lie on the couch and listen to classical music. A world unto themselves. Like my family, they had escaped with their lives to the New World. Unlike mine, they knew the arts and sciences beyond the ordinary. Peter tells us how certain top-notch German scientists high-tailed it to America, a group of physicists settling in upstate New York. Einstein and colleagues gathering for dinners to converse inside the tautologies of art and science. Einstein playing violin in a quartet. The safety of it. Music a way to weaken the gravity of imminent world war. "How was Einstein as a violin player?" Peter asked his mother. "Albert was good," she said. "Albert was good. But he had one fault. He couldn't count!" And Peter, who has taken up the art of storytelling, this night tells us over drinks a tale of an old man and a little boy. His German accent encircles the story, a world from which only the storyteller knows the exit.

CM:
Synesthesia

Flighty—this was how Hendon and I described his mother, Franny, heiress to an insurance fortune and historian of the Revolutionary War. A myopic redhead, thin as a rail, she spent whole days in bed, among her books. She encouraged my interest in poetry, praising in her clipped aristocratic accent Rimbaud's gift, in "Voyelles," for linking one sense to another, perceiving vowel sounds in terms of color: *Black A, White E* . . . Synesthesia was not a faculty to cultivate, according to her Swiss husband, as others might exploit the concept of limited liability, but a mark of genius, a subject about which he knew something: he was a cardiologist and researcher at Merck. We lived in the country, where genius was in short supply, so I spent all my free time at their house, hungry for culture—though Hendon dismissed his mother's writings, and his father's work interested us only as fodder for drug jokes. One night Franny invited my parents and another couple to dinner—and served no food. One by one they wandered into the kitchen to check the oven; after several drinks they retreated to our house, where my mother whipped up an omelet with eggs gathered from the chickens Hendon raised in the hut behind the barn. Another time Franny stood by the window in her living room, complaining to my mother about money. *But you're very rich,* said my mother. *How did you know?* said Franny, startled. Then she changed the subject, explaining why it was safe to leave her keys in the car. Right before her eyes a boy I knew climbed into the front seat and drove away. *Red I, Green U, Blue O.* . .

MB:
Fiction

He was the best teacher of fiction writing I ever saw in action. Years later, I told him as much at a lunch table. "You were the best," I said. "Yes," he said, "I know." Having no talent for fiction, I have figured out that a novel writer must engage and absorb the confidence of his characters. In fiction of a high order, as in life, character drives the plot. It was late in a bar in the Georgetown neighborhood of D.C. when two novelists and I decided to stay the night. We took bar stools, flanked by photos of soccer teams sponsored by the owner, and agreed we should each tell a story involving something that had happened that day. I was to go first. It was our intention that our inventiveness keep us awake even as the events themselves maintained the veracity of the mundane. Thus awarded the license to invent a surround for an event, I filled my story with pedestrians and activities and little shivers of experience. Then it was the turn of the judge's son, a respected novelist, and he too reported the events of his day but in engaging detail. John went third, and his story went on for some time, far longer than ours, yet it kept us at the edge of our seats. It seems his morning run had taken him through the zoo. He had stopped at a display cage in the herpetarium to watch a snake wrapped around a branch. After a lengthy period of immobility, the snake . . . moved. End of story. How could it have been as spellbinding with so small a plot? I must credit it to the sensory experience of the writer who could so feel the branch beneath his belly, the dull air against the sides of a cage, the vertical play of a creature whose landscape has been reduced to a cell. For it was the character of the snake that held us as the hour grew later. My friend John is a genius of the sensory. It is comic. It is tragic. He is, by now, all the characters of his stories. And I, destined to write the poetry of Prepostumous Absurdity, am still watching the snake.

CM:
Handicap

The copperhead was coiled around the cup on the ninth hole, and although my mother was deathly afraid of snakes she poked it with her putter, urging it to slither away. She was determined to complete the round—not to lower her handicap, which was of no interest to her, but because something started must come to its appointed end. The golf course was empty on that cool spring afternoon, and the branches of the willow trees hanging over the pond swayed in the wind, which laid cat's-paws on the surface of the waterhole into which our neighbor once hurled, one by one, all of his golf clubs and then his empty bag. The snake did not stir. Did my mother warn me not to remove the flag and lay it crosswise on the green, as I was about to do? She told the snake to get a move on, in the same insistent tone of voice she used in the morning to hurry me to school. Nor do I recall ever playing golf with her again. What remains in memory? The flickering tongue of the snake. A woman fierce in her resolve to record a number on her scorecard and initial it. The desire to invent another ending for a story, the meaning of which continues to elude me.

MB:
Frustration

I was the First Lieutenant, so he handed me the boa constrictor. I was the editor, so he read me the riot act. I was the columnist, so he threatened expulsion. I was of another race, so he said we could no longer play together. I was visiting, so they took my picture. I was a dad, so I started to notice the cost of things. I was fatherless and there was no going back. I was in town, and people knew it. Such are the defining moments of reports too complex to elaborate by microscope or telescope, for the serenity with which such moments may be cataloged belies the emotions at each circumstance. It's the music in my head that carries the details. In the Land of Memoir, there are fanfares, dirges, marches, even the exotic intervals of free form improvisation, but the verbal designations of emotion fall as flat as the rinky-dink choruses of "Name that Tune," that old-time quiz show that offered the illusion of taking part. My mother would say, about property in the Hamptons, "We could have bought it for a song, but who knew the words?" Likewise, our literary life is besieged by words without the music. Civilization has held doom at bay with the brainwork that follows every stimulus. Armies have devised new strategies—whether for living underground, the surgery of suicide bombings, or techie unraveling of the grid—by which to shred the underpinnings of language. Yet peace needs the feeling of peace. Chicken-and-egg.

CM:
Acronyms

The British Army is credited with naming the Improvised Explosive Devices (IEDs) used by the Provisional IRA during the Troubles in Northern Ireland. The armored vehicle known as an MRAP (Mine Resistant Ambush Protected), which took me in a convoy from the Forward Operating Base (FOB) at the airport outside Jalalabad to a poetry discussion in the city, was designed to withstand IEDs, the leading cause of American casualties in Afghanistan and Iraq. If necessity is the mother of invention, war is the father, and their issue can be counted in acronyms, technological advances (night-vision goggles, drones), and deaths. The Provisional Reconstruction Team (PRT) arranged the meeting with poets, writers, and journalists in the library of the Lincoln Center (LC), where I sat beside a colonel on his sixth tour in the war zone, a compact, graying man who told the Afghans that poetry was more useful now than guns. National Guardsmen from South Boston surrounded the building; after the event a local guard asked the colonel for the bullets in his pistol—which he gave him, except for the one in the chamber. *Now I've seen everything,* he said. Poetry is a way of seeing through the lens of a language tuned to music, linking one thing to another. The Viet Cong turned unexploded American ordnance into IEDs; Afghan mujahedeen did the same with duds dropped by the Soviet Air Force. It was too loud to talk in the MRAP. *I didn't know that Americans were the first astronauts who stepped on the moon,* said a poet at the LC. *I thought Russians were the first.* The FOB was named after one of the ten soldiers killed in a helicopter crash during a nighttime extraction in the mountains north of Jalalabad—Lieutenant Colonel Joseph J. Fenty, Jr. The trip back to the base seemed to take forever.

MB:
Carousel

Here before me, where I take a breather on a bench at the shopping mall, is the incarnation of if-and-when, chicken-and-egg, the wheel of history and the truth that, whether knowledgeable or ignorant of the past, we are doomed to repeat it. The proud horse, the poised jaguar, the see-it-all giraffe, the florid goat, the eager rabbit, the whiskery cat, the great gray elephant— like Keats's lovers on a vase, they can neither catch up nor gain space. I have for a while escaped the DNC and RNC during caucus week. The wheel turns, the platform of animals revolves, and here comes the menagerie. Those who disappear from view come back around. Jump on and off. Lean out to grab a ring and throw it into the clown's mouth. The dizziness is part of the excitement, like that of a roller coaster car hanging over the edge as it rounds a curve. The booby prize at the carnival games of chance used to be a pack of matches. Then it was a comb. We went along for the rides.

CM:
Todos Santos

The Bismarck palm outside the guest house, to which I had escaped from the caucuses, was thick with fruit, and El Chapo, the lamb named after the notorious drug lord, was sleeping at my feet while I wrote up my notes on the protest march through town. An American developer had drawn the ire of the fishermen, who feared the beach resort he was building would put them out of business. After the march broke up, I headed to the music festival, which ended on a dramatic note when the organizer, a retired rock star in his cups, took the stage to accuse the governor of corruption; soon he would flee the country on a private jet. The mission church was empty when I went in to pray for my late friend. The palm was named for Otto von Bismarck, the first chancellor of the German Empire; his diplomatic skills and practice of *realpolitik* were far removed from the bombast of the campaign in Iowa. Abandoned by its mother, the lamb cheerfully followed the owner's dogs around the compound. Some locals claimed the authorities had let the drug lord escape from prison so he could rein in the most violent members of the cartel. It was also said the developer had bought off one fishing cooperative; the other one blocked the dirt road to the resort to keep the construction workers out. Where the boats were hauled up on the beach, a shirtless man in white boots was cleaning fish, his knife gleaming in the sunlight. To launch a boat in such heavy surf requires an ability to read the waves, split-second timing, and courage in order to avoid being swept back into the rocks. There is no margin for error.

MB:
The Stakes

Even for the weekenders it was a gamble, betting the boat would stay upright, that someone would see them in trouble, that a passerby would have a rope, that the life jackets on the floor at the stern would be reached in time, and that their lives would not flash before their eyes as their brains searched for an exit. So, too, the "little old lady," who the salesman asserts drove the car "only on Sundays," gambled that the town souse was not out wheeling through a besotted eye-mist to a friend's for a day of drink. Statistics can tell us how many but not who. If 300 days a year the fish are where you an- chor, they may have been here yesterday. Watch the outboards motor out to the crowd, figuring an angler's navy knows where. Likewise, if an equal number of patients will breathe their last with or without treatment, your case is not determinant. Like auto sales and deep sea fishing, health care is a volume business. Blessings on those subversives who undercut the system. When our Yacht Club roped off half the beach, it was part of the gamble the rich make that the workers will not someday rise up. In the long term, democracy is a noble gamble by citizens who hope to beat the odds. Fated to relive the past, everyone loves an upset. We gamble repeatedly in youth on love because a new love is a fresh start.

CM:
Pearl Roundabout

Six white *dhow* sails rising from a pool of water and curling into the shape of a pearl, the symbol of Bahraini culture and the mainstay of its economy before the discovery of oil. There was a festive spirit in the air. Drivers tooted their horns in a four-beat rhythm to match the protesters' chant: *Down with Hamad*—the Sunni king whose family has ruled Bahrain since the eighteenth century. Blood was spilled the first time the Pearl Roundabout was cleared, three days after the start of the protests (seven coffins were displayed in honor of the men killed by the police), and the protesters circling the monument—doctors, nurses, students from a girls' school where a fight had broken out earlier in the day—expected more violence. From makeshift stages poets gave readings, public figures urged the crowd to stay calm in the face of provocations, a woman spoke about women's rights. Free food and tea were on offer—some called this the Popcorn Revolution. Two young women working for American financial companies volunteered to show me around. Ordinarily they spent their free time at the mall, but this was the place to be on a warm spring evening. Among the tents set up to house political parties, exhibit art about the martyrs, and provide medical services and information for the press was one for the writers' association. A novelist writing manifestos told me this was the first revolution with a schedule: Bahrain today, Saudi Arabia tomorrow, Kuwait the day after. He passed on a joke about Gaddafi: I'll shut off the power, he warned his rebellious people, and then you'll have to watch TV in the dark! It's not a joke, intoned another writer. He actually said it. Meantime militias hid truncheons under their robes, and police assembled by the palace. More blood would be shed before I arrived at the airport for my flight to Muscat. Saudi troops streamed across the causeway to restore order to the island. Riot police tore down the tents, arresting and torturing scores of protesters. When the Pearl Roundabout was razed to the ground, the protesters withdrew into their houses, and waited for the next spark.

MB:

The Paragraph as Witness: March 22, 2016, Brussels

Sometimes, anything more than a block of type is too precious. This time they blew up the airport and the subway. A revolution, whether of artists or true believers, beheads the pre-revolutionaries, who hitherto beheaded the founders, who earlier beheaded the natives. Those next in line slowly stock-piled fuel and devised a novel battle plan. The metaphor for the new warfare is the worm, tucked inside intention and the earth, blind to options, able to regenerate its body when hacked off beneath its head. The planarian flat-worm makes an ideal fifth column loyalist, able to remake itself from a sliver 1/300th its size, rebuilding its head and all its memories. Likewise, any nation writ into laws favoring the gentry can be undone by those who hope only to have their names on tombstones. Do I scowl? Very well then, I scowl. Where geography and religious dogma are determinant, we may resist with little more than facial expressions and obscene gestures. It's easy to see to which economic class high art belongs. Marcel Duchamp believed that art was either plagiarism or revolution. A possessed butchery persists above ground. As always, the invertebrates shall inherit the carnage. It is right to wonder what this has to do with prose vis-à-vis poetry. If I can fit the report into a paragraph that does not require the lyric's ambition for the tautological, it may disperse the killers and leave an opening for hope. If and when.

CM:
Nemesis

"I wonder what he meant by that," Metternich said upon learning that Talleyrand had died. For the architect of the Concert of Europe, the peace that held for a century until Archduke Ferdinand was assassinated in Sarajevo, no event occurs in a void, since Nemesis, agent of punishment for hubris, is ever vigilant. A commonplace in foreign policy circles is to argue that modern acts of terror—9/11, London, Madrid, Paris, San Bernardino, Istanbul, Brussels—obey a logic derived from the Old Testament story of David and Goliath: asymmetrical warfare can shape history as decisively as any battle plan drawn up at CENTCOM, not to mention works of literature and philosophy. But the distributer of fortune (the original meaning of Nemesis) is always lurking nearby, for good or ill. What I can report on my way to Mazar-e-Sharif, Noble Shrine, the first Afghan city to fall to U.S.-backed forces after 9/11, is that the idea of divine retribution seems to remain alive and well among the Taliban warriors who want to retake the city—site of battles and massacres, of love and loss, of faith and doubt: the subject of many poems by Rumi, who was born in the area. *You think you know what time it is*, he wrote. *It's time to pray.*

MB:
How We Survive

Or not. The lights in the sky may be intergalactic aircraft. Or not. I'm not licensed to pull the rug out from under guesswork. It is a solace to feel that one knows. Otherwise, our best maneuver is to change the odds. The day I was transferred from the infantry to a non-combat branch, I danced Dorothy around the kitchen. I had learned something from the icy roads and the leaky boats, back when I thought luck was on my side. I knew little of the skewed, the lopsided, and the misaligned. I knew little of chance, fortune, providence, or destiny. I knew nothing of the boundaries of one's class. We were primed to be conscripted into the masses of pawns, serfs, and slaves. So change the odds. Go it alone. During my army tour, a military adviser convinced me that a candidate for President, one who might employ nuclear weapons, might win. I secured our first passports: one for my wife and sons, another for myself. I would be traveling alone. I must have thought I'd return if needed. I am old enough now to know that escape beats sheltering in place. Short-termers know that payback has no end. He was prescient who said some things that happen to us are just bad luck.

CM:
Samangan

What are the odds of surviving a high-speed, head-on collision on a rural highway in Afghanistan? All I knew in the moments before a taxi passing a truck veered into our car was that it would hurt. My hosts, believing the Taliban would not disrupt our journey to a pre-Islamic shrine in Samangan, had advised me to wear a light-green *shalwar* and *kameez*, pajama-like trousers and a tunic; hence the man who pulled me from the car thought I was Afghan. A crowd had gathered, which suggested how long I had been knocked out, and they were yelling at the taxi driver. Both cars were totaled, and both of my hosts had broken their arms. A doctor from our group was cradling an unconscious boy, whose fate we would not learn. What did I know? Where the Hindu Kush meets the Central Asian steppe, Buddhists carved a monastery in a hillside, which the mujahedeen later used as a base in their fight against the Soviets. The walls and ceilings of the caves were black with soot, but they had survived the Taliban, unlike the Buddhas destroyed in Bamiyan. Our guide, accompanied by a guard armed with a Kalashnikov, knew less about the stupa than the doctor, who drove me through a sandstorm to a hospital in Mazar-e-Sharif. The Taliban's spring offensive was about to begin, and after an attack on Kabul, with suicide bombers and gunmen killing or wounding hundreds of men, women, and children, its Department for the Prevention of Civilian Casualties warned drivers "to follow all traffic rules." A sense of humor goes a long way in a war zone.

MB:
My Knees

I blame them for my being bow-legged. When my friend Frank put off replacing his crumbling knees until Medicare, he grew increasingly shorter. A tall bow-legged Italian and a short bow-legged Ukrainian—we heard our wives laughing as we walked ahead of them. Frank registered the pain for years while he waited. His fortitude trumps my uncontrolled descent down a bare, rigid stairway in southern Illinois onto a cement floor where I landed on my knees among pears, grapes, and oranges. I had started down while balancing a suitcase, a bag of books and a fruit basket, missed a step early, and thereafter spun a flurry of parts until I hit. The landing ripped everything off my knees. I had no legs, but I had ankles, which were enough with which to drive the four hours home, where the doctor on call noted with mild amusement that they didn't usually see "both knees at once." A week in a chair, a week in the hospital, and four months in a hospital bed at home. I knew, even as I spun down the steps, that landing on my knees at the bottom of a staircase was preferable to a head-first descent. Call it good luck, why not? Wearing hinged leggings, I looked like RoboCop in pajamas. Like a sort of ancient toddler, I moved from a walker to crutches to a cane. It took a year before I could hurry across a street. Now I'm a geezer for whom drivers slow, but then I was just another member of the flock the young like to scatter. They call it black comedy when you can laugh afterwards.

CM:
Immunity

This votive offering, a gold-leaf plaque with an embossed arm, was supposed to ease the pain in my swollen wrists—a parting gift from a woman who set fire to my imagination. No one knows why the body rebels against itself, said the doctor, prescribing ten pills a day and weekly injections to keep my autoimmune system in check. As a child I was taunted for crying, and now I wonder if my determination to keep my cool was what triggered a reaction that makes it hard for me to shake hands. According to tradition, the healing properties of this votive (*tama* in Greek, signifying both prayer and object) derive from a story about John of Damascus, a Church Father and defender of icons: how as vizier to the caliph he was falsely accused of treachery, the penalty for which was the amputation of his hand; how it was miraculously restored to him as he prayed before an icon of the Theotokos, the Mother of God; how he went on to write hymns as well as treatises on faith and heresy, dragons and ghosts. This *tama* hangs with a rosary from the desk drawer in which I keep alcohol swabs for the shots I give myself on Wednesday mornings, this time recalling a woman named for the huntress who killed her companion. O, O, O…

MB:
Gravitas

It was our Northwest cross-the-street Navy vet Lew who, after his stroke, having showed me the museum cases, the chest of money, and the "Do Not Resuscitate" note on the refrigerator, taught himself to write exquisite script with his other hand. He and his spouse Helen collected Chinese and Japanese miniature perfume bottles, Native American arrowheads, Oriental jade carvings, exotic coins, and florid necklaces from the world over—all displayed at home, not for public viewing. A couple so private that Dorothy and I would come to be for years the only people invited inside their house. Asked to a July 4th barbecue by more social citizens, he said, "We don't do that." Nor did he travel. He had had his fill of it in the Navy. We, on the other hand, to spend time in our Northwest retreat, drove 2,000 miles each way for thirty years before our summer friends passed away, feisty Helen having hung on for years in a bedridden semi-trance from which she nevertheless woke at the sound of my voice. I think back to the night before our first turn-around to drive home from Port Townsend. I had lingered inside the car in the dark to catch my breath when there was a knock on the driver's side window. It was Lew, whom we hardly knew, handing me an antique jade figurine of a dog for good luck. I have been given at times the New Age magic seeds, the healing scent packet, and the prayers of strangers, but it is Old World *gravitas* that protects us. He and Helen had it. Amulets have it and rituals accumulate it. A poet must earn it. Some facts are raw.

CM:
The Cosmos Club

What triggered my tears was not the news of a third friend's death within a week but the recording of Dylan singing "Knockin' on Heaven's Door" on Frank's memorial website. I often turned to Frank for political advice, and when he invited me to dine with him at the Cosmos Club on Embassy Row I was the rube in a shapeless suit and unpolished shoes. He ordered a single malt, neat, and as he schooled me in the ways of Washington, tracing a history of connections between art and diplomacy—two fields in which he claimed no expertise but passion—an image floated into my mind of an old mariner sailing a ship into port. *That long black cloud is coming down,* Dylan sang as I read the tributes of friends and family. Fairport Convention, Eric Clapton, the Grateful Dead, U2, the Alarm, Guns N' Roses, all covered the song written for the soundtrack of *Pat Garrett & Billy the Kid*—which Sam Pekinpah left out of his preview of the film. My favorite version was recorded by the Scottish musician Ted Christopher after the school massacre at Dunblane, with Mark Knopfler on guitar and a children's choir singing the refrain. Dylan allowed Christopher to add a verse and the first lines of Psalm 23 to the Dunblane version, which topped the charts for Christmas week 1996; the royalties were donated to charity. *This town will never be the same,* the Scotsman sang. *The Lord is my shepherd I shall not want.* How I miss Frank.

MB:
Why

After he died, I wrote poems about my father because I still knew him. First I brought him to life, floating face up in a coffin, imagining in this way an afterlife "...after the fact, / in a dream, in a probable volume, in a / probable volume of dreams..." My defenses were fantasy and hypothesis. I gave him more life, remembered him in his easy chair, "legs propped straight, the head tilted back" as he rested a weak heart. In my mind, I returned him to his Ukraine and said, "I just want to be happy again. That's / what I was, happy, maybe am, you would know." In dreams and awake, I saw him everywhere and pulled away, thinking, "We must stay away from our fathers, / who have big ears." I would go back to tell him, "I think that light's a sheet for the days, / which we lose. Then we go looking." I came to see that the project, if it was a project, was impossible. I compared an "adolescent weeping willow" to the son who could never know how it felt to be his father because the son was "only a boy." Twenty-five years after the floating coffin of a fantasy, I stood again at the burial, tracked it moment by moment, and added it up: "My father's grave. I will never again. / Never. Never. Never. Never. Never": the finality of Lear's words, said above the body of his daughter, upended so that now a son speaks them over his father. The injury from which one might have pulled the scab, the wound into which one might have poured salt—art can do more than reshape pain. We invent our survival.

CM:
Curriculum

The English textbook used by ISIS includes this example to explain the present continuous tense: *I'm visiting some wounded mujahedeen in hospital. Would you like to come? Oh! I'd love to.* For an exercise in revision students are ordered to fill in the blank: *People who commit _____ in Islamic State are stoned.* And from a lesson titled "From Raqqa to Nigeria," which focuses on usage, not geography: *Would you like to come with me to watch the applying stone limit on a couple of adultery in the city centre this afternoon? Oh! That's a good idea.* The Iraqi journalist who sent me the curriculum warned: *Children make brutal recruits.* In my childhood, during the Vietnam War, I was recruited for the soccer, tennis, and track teams; when the draft ended in my sophomore year of high school, I was spared the moral decisions faced by able-bodied upperclassmen who could not secure student deferments. To fight or flee—this was a question I did not need to answer, which must have influenced my life in ways I cannot discern. Imagine an English teacher in Raqqa exploring the future tense with students terrified of the Predator drones circling overhead. It is hard to pay attention to a man with a thick accent when you are listening with every fiber of your being for warplanes. The future is a savage recruiter.

MB:
No Theory

Standing on a balcony in Paris during World War II, my uncle Al looked like the symbol of safe heroism. His khaki undershirt suggested the sort of exotic travel that includes a temporary freedom from American Puritanism. He would bring back a German rifle. War souvenirs included brass swastikas, Lugers—even, in our town, an American Jeep mailed home in parts. There existed, in that time, what one might think of as ethical ballast: small misbehaviors to be tossed overboard in a storm. It was the privilege of the savior, not of the saved, to capture a memento. Drawings and diaries of children in the Nazi camps notwithstanding, idealistic pacifists must live with their pie-in-the-sky notion that the Jews will benefit from inaction. During a pleasant lunch outdoors, the writer told me that the Nazis had offered to allow humanitarian workers into the camps to administer to the prisoners on one condition: that they not help the prisoners escape. "What would you do," he asked? I said I'd promise not to help the prisoners escape, and then I'd help them escape. He waved a forefinger side to side to suggest that one's word is one's bond. Just as my Ukrainian father had to flee from both the Czar and the Bolsheviks, I have navigated between the pacifists and the war hawks. "No theory will stand up to a chicken's guts being cleaned out ..." wrote the poet David Ignatow, "no theory that does not grow sick at the odor escaping." We stomach what we have to.

CM:
Politics

The stench from the dead squirrel lodged in the undercarriage of the car made my head spin in the summer heat until I opened the hood to pour boiling water over its remains, which I could not hook with a coat hanger; maggots feeding on its flesh spilled into the street, and when I tugged on the bits of fur hanging from a pair of holes under the radiator guts and gristle, bones and more maggots, all spilled through my hands. How a squirrel ended up in the engine is anybody's guess. I could not wash its odor from my fingers—a common experience, it seemed to me, for those who work on campaigns for the highest office in the land. In the forum on national security, for instance, when the Republican presidential nominee, who claimed to know more about fighting terrorism than the generals, argued that the military judicial system did not exist, I saw in my mind's eye the squirrel's mangled limbs and smelled again its rotting flesh, pieces of which dripped from the car for hours after I had closed the hood. In *The Cantos* Ezra Pound likened politicians to wet coal, mistaking his poetic vocation for political insight. No telling what will become of this country after the votes are tallied up. Maggots can survive almost any apocalypse.

MB:
Love > Fear

How happy we were in the interstices, crannies and fissures. We found safety in trenches and caves, in basements and forests. The cracks and gaps shielded the luckiest of us when armies fought house-to-house. If we feared that cruelty would trump compassion, that even in peacetime there would be little backing off of the war hawks and loudmouths, that the desperate were destined to seek salvation in the end-times of the abyss, it was greatly modified by song and dance, by the goodness of strangers. While the Republican candidate was plundering his charity for personal legal fees and commissioning a humongous portrait that still could not contain his ego, while a Senator's daughter was scheming to price gouge the users of lifesaving injections, and while the ideologues were pretending to be thinkers, we were secretly kissing, necking in the back row, putting our hands all over one another, and proving, as the songwriter said, that love is greater than fear. My one-time student, a calligrapher, had a few days to live when he said, "You know, I have had a great life. Twice in my life, I have been in bed with a beautiful woman I loved." Our big shots may live in an inferno. We need not. I had walked a mile down a highway in Memphis to find something to eat at a mini-mart where the cashier asked the raggedly clothed, beat-up, homeless habitué if he was having "a good day." "*Every* day is a good day," he replied. Forgive me for always opting-in, but you can't beat that.

CM:
Greed

The first sting felt as if I had caught my ankle on barbed wire. Then another and another as a colony of yellow jackets swarmed around me, stinging my calves, thighs, back, arms, neck, and eyebrow. I had disturbed their nest while weeding under the hedge; when I dropped the hoe and bounded up the front steps the wasps followed until I slammed the door shut behind me. Thirty or more welts rose on my body, my head began to spin, my breathing grew labored; hence the EpiPen prescribed for me in the emergency room, which I must carry everywhere. But there was something else: in a recital that night at the senior center my younger daughter sang "Over the Rainbow," her clear high voice lined with the knowledge, or so it seemed to me as I recovered from the allergic reaction, that while pain is our common inheritance music can be a balm for the afflicted and love lifts the soul. She sang it again this summer, with a jazz beat, to close the memorial service for a colleague struck down in the prime of life, a scholar of medieval theater who had introduced performance studies to the discipline. For the duration of the song I was distracted from my despair over the drift of our politics, which had convinced me that we also share a propensity for greed. My EpiPen, for example, had expired, and insurance would not cover the exorbitant cost of a new one. But sunlight streamed through the windows of the performance hall as Abby sang, *Why, oh, why, can't I?* My colleague's friends and family cried. I was not alone in wanting more.

MB:
Moving Pictures

I could not pass up the second-hand CD by the heavy metal band "Surrender Dorothy" from the urban sidewalk vendor of old music. It was my wife Dorothy, at four years of age, treated to the "The Wizard of Oz" by her mother, who became terrified when the green Wicked Witch of the West threatened the movie girl: *I'll get you, my pretty.* The song "Over the Rainbow" that welcomes us into the story of Dorothy Gale is the farm girl's wish to find a better place, but for parents it is a song that can tear at the heart of anyone who wishes to save the children. Even second-hand pain, come from far-off, can feel intimate. They show you the children atop the garbage heaps looking for something to eat or sell. They tell you of the children blind from carpet-sewing in bad light. They report the kidnappings and the numbers sold into servitude by desperate families. They add the photo of the ten-year-old, struggling to lift an Uzi, conscripted into a civil war. For a piece of bread. For one day more. My son Nathan sings of a couple with no job, on the road with their belongings, in which the driver says, "Me and the Missus had another bad year. We know there's a rainbow, but it ain't around here." We want children to prolong our experience of innocence. Parenthood is, in two ways, a holding action. Music always wins because it is impenetrable.

CM:
Glass

The anniversary of Kristalnacht was dawning when my daughter Hannah called from Strasbourg in despair over Donald Trump's looming election. This was the first of several calls she made that day, trying to understand this betrayal of American ideals. *Bad things come in threes,* the French say. I) On 9 November 1938 Nazi Stormtroopers destroyed thousands of Jewish homes, schools, hospitals, and synagogues, littering the streets with broken glass, and killed or imprisoned tens of thousands of people. 2) Fifty-five years later to the day, Croatian forces destroyed the Old Bridge in Mostar, a sixteenth-century Ottoman engineering marvel. And 3) a campaign of hatred, bigotry, and misogyny had just delivered a demagogue to the White House. It turns out that democracy is as fragile as love. What to tell Hannah, who was studying abroad in preparation for a possible career in the Foreign Service? That working for the government may inspire moral questions that are difficult to answer? Between the German invasion of Poland and the Anglo-French declaration of war two days later, the city of Strasbourg was evacuated and remained empty until France fell; many young men and women who returned were pressed into service in the German Army—a fate they did not live down, if they survived the war. Hillary Clinton was supposed to break the glass ceiling that keeps women from the highest office in the land. What I heard over the phone line was the sound of grief shattering the heart of my daughter, who was determined to be brave.

MB:
Sarajevo, 1983

The festival concluded at a banquet. We were given certificates and kisses. At an outsized wooden rectangle fit together by long tables, I was seated across from the mayor, while the Russian poet was seated with another official at some distance. The mayor sang the praises of the United States to me, honoring my nation's participation in World War II. The American presidency, he said, is an important international position and must be respected. He repeated, in several ways, that the presidency, the very office, is so important that it must always be respected. I knew by then the code, the conversational strategy, still necessary in Eastern Europe: obliquity wrapped in a way that there could be no response, since any response might expose one's satiric intention. I knew he was saying, "Your president is a jerk." As the banquet ran down, my translator took me to a tavern frequented by young poets. They spoke little English, and I spoke no Serbo-Croatian. She explained that I was an American poet, at which point a young man lifted his glass as if in toast and declared, in English, *"Fuck Reagan!"* He asked the translator to find out if I was a Republican or a Democrat. "Neither," I said, "Independent." Again he raised his glass, this time with a look of glee, and said, *"Ah, Anarchista!"* With a clink of our glasses, he conscripted me into the struggle against the bully puppets of the villainous.

CM:
Sarajevo, 1993

The muscles in my lower back, torn on my first reporting trip to the besieged city, flared up again on Thanksgiving. Hunched over, I shuffled from the dining room table to the couch in the same pain I experienced in the basement of a house rented to humanitarians, which for one long day and night was the target of Serbian gunners in the hills surrounding Sarajevo. During a lull in the bombardment, I went upstairs and out onto the balcony to survey the damage—dust rising from the detonations, an acrid smell of gunpowder, the distant thudding of artillery. A bullet flew by my head, lodging in the lintel, and as I dove through the door, twisting under the weight of my Kevlar vest, my back seized up—an injury that took weeks to heal, and then only partially, becoming a form of muscle memory that returns whenever the weather changes. War is what I remember most vividly of my walk in the sun; if it determines the key in which I love, grieve, and write, then these words carry overtones of the rounds that landed outside the house, in which we were debating what to read in the intervals between barrages. History? Poetry? Erotica? Our meal by candlelight was a joyous occasion, despite the humanitarian fare, and I was grateful to record the stories of men and women who worked long hours helping those who had lost everything. What did they decide was best to read? Erotica, of course. Desire trumps all.

MB:
Mr. Berdan, 1954

It was our tall, easygoing high school English teacher Mr. Berdan who abruptly stopped talking about the lesson and said to the class, "You know how people are always telling you these are the best years of your lives? Don't you believe it. It gets better and better." I'm pretty sure he was in love when he said it. You know the saying, "Love conquers all." Later we heard the Beatles sing, "All you need is love." For whose love does a sniper wait patiently for a kill? He may sit for hours, wrapped in camouflage, his heartbeat slow, his scope magnifying the distance. The man running gets it. The woman with a sack of vegetables gets it. The child with the water bucket gets it. The rifle crack could be a dead bolt snapping shut. The Kalashnikov is famously reliable but infamously inaccurate, so the combatant sets it on automatic, hoping to hit someone. The nervous policeman, mistaking a wallet for a gun, takes as many shots as he can get off in a burst. He hasn't time to apply the acronym BRASS, which reminds marksmen to breathe-relax-aim-slack-squeeze. The sniper, on the other hand, has license to choose targets, to shoot or not, to move or stay. If he fired at you and missed, know that you meant nothing to him beyond an abstract tally. It may be deathly quiet after a shot. Perhaps a bird twitters to hear a rustle where he reloads. He will say he desires peacetime, while for him his score will rise but things will never get better. Shooting from a standing position, the trainee leans forward. If one misses the target entirely, a red flag will be waved to embarrass the shooter. They call it "Maggie's Drawers." If it was a dull day on the range, we'd shoot wide of the target on purpose to draw forth Maggie's Drawers. Nothing was said about deciding not to shoot.

CM:
The Art of Diplomacy

This bowl made of brass casings from bullets fired in Sarajevo was presented to me after a reading in a café in Amman. An intervention during the question & answer period by a Jordanian official, whose fiery speech, in unaccented English, accusing the Embassy of ignoring protocol in arranging this event without permission from the Ministry of Foreign Affairs, bewildered our delegation; the hostess's gesture was thus a welcome distraction. Our control officer, a suave diplomat fluent in Arabic, Russian, and Spanish, approached the official, not to mollify him but to explain that he needed no permission to showcase writers. I thanked our hostess for the gift, which I planned to set on my desk next to a bullet acquired in a market at the end of the war in Bosnia, which was painted black with a gold illustration of a minaret. Outside the café was a brown sedan covered with books for sale, which a young man with a ponytail drove from town to town to encourage his compatriots to read. An introduction to Roethke's poetry caught my eye, perhaps because I had visited a Zen garden on Bainbridge Island, formerly the swimming pool in which the Garden-Master drowned. He believed a *lively understandable spirit* would entertain him again before his heart seized up underwater; and as I meditated on the moss-covered boulders arranged in groups of two and three on the raked sand I recalled his counsel: *Be still. Wait.*

MB:
Enough

A brass bowl made from spent ammunition. A single bullet painted. The re-purposed leftovers of battles. We embrace that craft and art that expresses at once the surface and underside of life. I am a sucker for the moment in the Cole Porter song that begins, "Every time we say goodbye, I die a little" when the singer hears a lark sing of romance but notes "how strange the change from major to minor" as the pianist replicates the change in the har-mony. We cannot but sing the heartbreak of parting. For some, it's the guilt of a survivor. We who were born to better odds than others nonetheless must live with dirges, even as we salute life. I am reminded of what is nec-essary by the simple dinner toast of a movie father, Joseph Cutter in "The Forger": "Life is hard and things go wrong. May we always have enough." In a cruel time, we wait inside ourselves for whatever is coming. It is up to us to say when enough is enough.

CM:
Inauguration

The British writer described his plays as propositions, designed to help audiences understand what was happening to them. The election of Donald Trump, for example, he regarded as an aftershock of 9/11, the Iraq War, and the financial crisis; and though he professed to have no interest in writing about the reality TV star—*It's impossible to satirize Donald Trump*, he explained, *because he is self-satirizing*—the crowd in Rajasthan peppered him with questions about the man he called *non-factual*. Fact: It was standing room only at the opening event of the Jaipur Literature Festival, the kind of turnout Trump would falsely claim for his inauguration. The transition of power in my country I marked from far away, imagining that distance might lessen my anxiety about the rise of authoritarianism—a recurring theme in the panel discussions at the festival. The playwright turned to his writing process: it was critical for him to get words down on paper, no matter how foolish they might sound. Some days he told himself to just write rubbish, confidant that the next day he would find bits of gold in the dross. This was how he silenced his internal critic, who knew all the ways in which he would fail even before he took up his pen. Tell that to Trump.

MB:
Residual Reality

Maybe the play really is the thing, beyond Hamlet's use of a dumbshow to confirm the legitimacy of his motive for revenge. Is our enjoyment, as Aristotle would have it, a catharsis: a mass phlebotomy to rid the body of toxic government? That is, can we apply the high-sounding term "tragedy"—i.e., a fall from a high place—to any self-delusional head of a rabid clan? It seems threats are as American as apple pie. Lose a few games, and the fans want your head. Blow a call near the end of a tight match, and the losing coach never lets up. Fans of no appreciable athletic ability savage young men for dropping a pass. Today the mob has found higher game. Say anything thoughtful, and the Internet arsonists coalesce. The photographer Robert Heinecken had his ashes sent to me in a salt shaker labeled "residual reality." He was not surprised by the phenomenon. Vietnam, then the residual reality. Iraq, and the residual reality. Now Syria and its residual reality. Come back, paraphotographer Heinecken, who unstapled copies of *Time*, then superimposed, upon a deodorant ad, the image of a female ARVN fighter, a cartridge belt across her chest, carrying two bloody heads, after which he reassembled the magazines and returned them to the store shelves. Truth has layers, and one of them is residual reality. Look again. Look underneath. If we are but players on a stage, it is time for the mimes to speak.

CM:
Stage Directions

The Iraqi director's decision to cut out all the dialogue in his staging of the American play did not rise to the level of a diplomatic incident—though the State Department funding leant an official air to the seething anger of the playwright, who viewed the production in a digital video conference room at Foggy Bottom. Her father, an Iraqi civil engineer, had moved to this country before her birth, and who could blame her for regarding the staging directions through the lens of his stories? Her reputation derived from a suite of monologues she had composed for the women of his homeland, in defiance of the ancient impulse to silence them; the director's argument for choosing the language of dance over what she had written fell on deaf ears. Impossible to escape history, even in a land oriented toward the future, much less one riven by sectarian violence. The pantomime I watched through the darkened windows of the armored car that took me to a pavilion in Baghdad's Green Zone—a shepherd leading his flock of lambs through the crowded market—dated back to the Mesopotamian origins of language, when merchants carved into cuneiform figures tallying their losses and gains. The intelligence report that terrorists planned to strike during my lecture was not conveyed to me until after I had returned to the Embassy. Ignorance is bliss, I would have joked if I had summoned the wherewithal to speak.

MB:
Black Ink

While we waited for the American poet to show up, his Japanese wife waited with us in their restaurant. They had come to Boston from Kyoto where he had an ice cream shop. After an hour passed without the poet, she brought forth a sumi-e set and painted for each of us, with a learned spontaneity, a Japanese character, each signifying what she saw in that person. We can't help but wonder what others think of us. I felt affection in her selection of characters. Her calm regard may be contrasted with the manic torture of a young poet. One might like to be thought special, but when a deeply afflicted student, hearing voices and having put out a cigarette on his cheek, arrives at your door to tell you that you are a god, that you can fly, and that you can make yourself invisible, what do you say? I said I was just a friend. He said he had walked the streets on Easter Sunday, wanting to be crucified. He told me he had seen a man burned alive. I asked if he thought that what he had seen was only in his head. He sat silent, unable to answer. His reality was the only reality. It was insular, as convincing as the self-delusion of political windbags. We have learned to live under threat, encircled by a barrage of stimuli and exponential change. We labor to maintain a calm regard. Let mime and dance do their best. We are walking against the wind. It takes our breath away.

CM:
Shock Wave

No sooner did I say that it felt as if we could be driving in an almost normal city than a car bomb detonated three hundred meters away, in Baghdad's Karrada neighborhood, killing four policemen at a checkpoint and wounding eight. A shock wave broke over our armored vehicle, momentarily deafening me. Flames shot up between the buildings we passed, and black plumes of smoke rose from the street littered with the burning hulks of cars. *Faster*, said our Iraqi host, a poet-professor who had a story from the war with Iran: how he was dragooned from a classroom during an exam, before he could finish checking his answers, and ordered to the front; how he deserted with two friends in the midday heat, entered what he called an artificial forest, and met a security agent, who gave them water to drink; how his plea to visit his mother did not prevent his arrest. When he escaped from detention, his father took him back to the front and begged the commander to let him go. *Careful*, the poet told the driver. The blare of sirens everywhere. The city was on high alert: the bombing marked Saddam Hussein's birthday; a village dating from the time of the Sumerians had just been retaken from ISIS; more suicide bombers were likely on the way. The guards at the Babylon Hotel took their time inspecting our vehicle. My ears are still ringing.

MB:
Living Dangerously, 2017

I have learned safety from my son, Jason, a trained Ninja. In the security contingent for the Dalai Lama's visit to New York City, he was instructed in the event of trouble to pull the Dalai Lama inside, bolt the door, and let the others fend for themselves. Jason says you do not know a martial art until you can defend yourself from a surprise attack by three people. Hence, one is prepared for contingencies, as in my hometown we were ready for a scrap, but the first rule of ninjitsu is, "If you have to fight, you've lost." It's awareness to the max: when trouble starts, you saw it coming and are not there. What is too easily called "mindfulness" is but a wimpy posture in a war. Besieged by the news, our ears ringing from a rule of lies, what, then, shall we do? It was in Chicago when, crossing a lawn, late for an exam, I saw a crowd lining the street and stuck my head in to see the Queen of England pass by, followed by Prince Philip, whom, judging by the applause and murmurs, the onlookers much preferred. Had we royalty, even a delusional narcissist, if elected by a hoodwinked mob, would have to go on bended knee to be scolded by Mom.

CM:
Sundowning

My mother's agitation at dusk cannot be treated, only accommodated, according to the doctor who diagnosed her dementia. Nor can my father convince her that they are not checking into a different hotel every night; when he refuses to look for her two imaginary cats, which she knows for a fact have escaped from the house, she lashes out at him, sometimes with her fists. I have grown used to her repetition of questions and inability to remember the names of her grandchildren. But this return to violence, which fueled my childhood terrors, is unsettling, just as the breaking news from Washington leaves me in a state of constant anxiety. If it is the poet's prerogative to view personal tragedies through the lens of politics, more so in a time of uncertainty, then I regard my mother's syndrome as symptomatic of the national malaise. What triggers her anger? Perhaps the fading light, which marks the end of any empire, when gossip, failure, and the potential consequences of broken alliances govern debates in the streets and halls of power. I picture my mother on the deck, seething at my father, who is flipping channels to find out who lawyered up today. Somewhere in the tall grass at the edge of sight is a red-tailed hawk swooping in on a pair of cats.

MB:

"Ceci n'est pas une pipe."

Who better than the Belgian surrealist René Magritte to have framed "The Treachery of the Image" that so deceives the mind? The inconvenient truth is that *Un portrait de Trump ne sera pas Trump.* So, too, the later assemblages of the surrealist Joseph Cornell are a blueprint for the Funhouse of the Trumps, now that there is already more than enough for the carnival. Let the rooms be accurately named: The Breezeway of Cyberbullying, The Gangway of Tweets, Memorial for the Stiffed Workers, The Great Fake *Time* Cover Exhibit, Portrait Gallery of a Synthetic Family, The Wall of Scurrilous Lawyers, The Parlor of Misogyny, Catalog Exhibit of the Underhanded Proxies (a.k.a., The Clan of the Cat's-Paws), Atrium Illumination of the Spouse's Contract with the Devil, Exit Parade of The Obeisant Senators. In the gift shop: remaindered diplomas from Trump University. On the façade, a "Make America Mine" pennant. Next door, a research institute to study the triangulation of narcissism, hubris and delusion. "Finally," say the researchers, "a subject." Never mind the subtler overlaps of sanity and insanity. Intent is not the issue, but a shameful helplessness. Ah René, to a twit nothing is anything.

CM:
Slow Under Construction

The Berlin Wall was still standing in the summer of 1989 when a friend and I began to translate *Ralentir travaux*, a magnetic book of poems by André Breton, Paul Éluard, and René Char, which they had composed on a driving tour of the Vaucluse region in southern France. In the spring of 1930, with the Surrealist movement splintering over debates about the relationship between poetry and revolution, Breton and Éluard disappointed in love, and the French economy teetering on the edge of the Great Depression, the poets traded lines in a spirit of camaraderie, listening for what Char called "words liberated but suffering." They took their book title from a sign along a river warning drivers of road repairs ahead, and I came to think of their book as a series of collisions between dream and reality. We finished our translation not long before a crowd of East Berliners took sledgehammers to the Wall, which had seemed impregnable; as one political order gave way to another I recalled Marx's dictum: *History repeats itself first as tragedy, then as farce.* Fast forward to Trump's systematic dismantling of American institutions, alliances, and democratic traditions. *What follows resembles what leaves,* the poets wrote. If only.

MB:
W2IDK

Back when amateur radio was still amateur, when a novice wanting to be accepted by the grownups had to build a transmitter and power supply but was relieved from the more difficult task of building a receiver, we made fun of the single-sideband users whose voices sounded over a normal receiver like Donald Duck. We laughed at the squawking, allowing it no credit for using only half a frequency, and easily abandoned any attempt to adjust the beat frequency oscillator to land so precisely on the signal that we might make out the voice. Does this sound technical? It was primitive compared to amateur TV, bouncing signals off the moon, and the general turn toward the interplanetary that would come later. Now when I think of early single-sideband, I think not of a Disney character but of Donald Trump, a one-man squawk team, a whiner I would imagine wearing a diaper had I not seen pictures of him pasted to his tie. If Baby Trump had been required to build a transmitter and power supply, not from a kit but from parts and tools to match a schematic, would he not now be more than a brat? CQ, CQ, is anyone out there? QRM? QRN? Interference? Static? QSA? Am I getting through? QSL. Please acknowledge. I am the ghost of W2IDK, the boy who stayed up after midnight to listen to the dark.

CM:
Image Analysis

A photograph released by the North Korean government after it test-fired a second intercontinental ballistic missile in a matter of weeks shows the Supreme Leader Kim Jong-un observing the launch through binoculars, his elbows propped on a map affixed to a wooden desk in an outdoor command post near the Chinese border. Image analysis of the map reveals the trajectory of the missile, which flew for forty-five minutes before landing in the Sea of Japan. This means that the Hermit Kingdom may soon be able to strike an American city with a nuclear-tipped weapon. Further analysis reveals that as the news broke Donald Trump was playing golf—a constant feature of his presidency; his tweet before North Korea tested its first missile—"It won't happen"—would shape the remarks I was preparing for a literary festival in Seoul, which were inspired by the last lines of a poem by Chanho Song: *I wonder who removed the pin from this apple. / It's red enough to explode at any moment.* There are thousands of artillery batteries on the North Korean side of the border; a shell fired from there will land in the South Korean capital in forty-five seconds. One theory of the etymology for the golfing word of warning *Fore!* is that it derives from what artillerymen would shout to the infantry at the front: *Beware before!* One errant shot can ruin everything.

MB:
Facial Recognition

Side views of the good-looking often reveal uneven cheeks or dispropor-
tionate noses. One hears the plea to photographers to "take my good side."
X & Y, though less handsome and beautiful than other actors, were said to
be the more photogenic. I can, however, spot no difference between the good
and bad sides of the Trump-Kushner family. Side-to-side and front-to-back,
swathed in sanitary clothing, faces planed of affect, the son, daughter and
son-in-law display the stare of a cult. If one hesitates to think the leader's
followers victims of mind-control, one must acknowledge the sway of a guru
whose one goal is to accumulate money by any means. The lock-step, the
miserliness, the crusade against exposure—all underlie a financial chicanery
intrinsic to cults. What does our president see through the heavy makeup
of showbiz? Do his ad-libs mean that he is all-in for war, or are they just
chubby bluster? Does he know that his face can be washed out by the flash
of a camera? Has he heard of Narcissus, who stared at his reflection in a
pool until he died? I sit rapt among the night news viewers beset by the
leader of the lookalikes, the late show comedic banter, and the edgy guess-
work of the explainers.

CM:
Charlottesville

I spent a summer at the university, studying French and the literature of the American Renaissance. My girlfriend took classes in art history, and we befriended a young couple who served mint juleps to introduce us to the South. His father was a psychiatrist pioneering a new therapy for depression, taking his patients to the football stadium to run around the track, and her father was a lawyer in Carter's Department of Justice. One night she drank so much that she passed out, and I had to remove her contact lenses. On the 4th of July, during the fireworks display, S. and I made love on a hillside below Jefferson's house at Monticello. I do not recall the statue to Robert E. Lee, though I have a vivid memory of my English professor repeatedly lighting his pipe during a lecture on *Moby Dick*. Nor could I know that on her return to California S. would betray me with her father's Norwegian friend. Virginia's flora was new to her, so she didn't recognize the leaves of poison ivy she used to wipe herself one day when she went for a run in the woods and had to pee. Her allergic reaction was severe, a rash and blisters spreading from her genitals to her entire body; she endured a week of prednisone, cold showers, and misery before she could leave her sickbed, by which time she was in a deep depression. Anything could set her off, and then anything did.

MB:
Charlottesville, 08/12/2017

Once upon a time, I'd like to say, there was a salve to soothe my sunburned back, the aftermath of shirtless play in the woods, so red hot that walking down the stairs caused great pain just by wrinkling the blisters. Later, when Castro took Havana right after my friend Lew and I had arrived for a hint of Hemingway, we fled to Miami Beach to sun, from where I later took a Trailways bus north, having to pour hand lotion down my shirt to ease the burn that had been magnified by the waters of Biscayne Bay. I think back to the routine grade school colds and small fevers that brought forth a spread of Vick's VapoRub under my polo shirt. I trusted my school nurse and Smith Brothers cough drops. College mono meant something to swig, even in class, its pharmacological name cloaking the alcohol in it. There was valve oil for my cornet and Vaseline for its slides, neatsfoot oil to soften a baseball glove. Once upon a time, we had an ointment for everything and many of us bled for our nation, as we do today. R.I.P., Heather Heyer.

CM:
Tent City

Donald Trump's admission that his desire for better TV ratings governed the timing of his decision to pardon Sheriff Joe as Hurricane Harvey made landfall on the Gulf Coast brought to mind the televised footage, in black-and-white, of the hurricane that swept our family house out to sea. Even at the age of five I knew that nothing would ever be the same. But who can comprehend the scale of any tragedy? It was raining on the winter day I visited the looted museum and memorial site of the Jasenovac concentration camp in Slavonia, and my Croatian guide could not wait to return to Zagreb. She was sick of hearing about her countrymen's crimes against humanity— the film she had been forced to watch (her words) on a school trip had made her retch—and she was fond of pointing out that even Germans had tired of talking about Nazis. The cattle cars were intact; also the mounds of earth beneath which some 80,000 murdered Serbs, Jews, and Roma were buried. The museum would be rebuilt. Sheriff Joe referred to the tent city in which he housed prisoners as a concentration camp. In the summer of 2011, he tweeted, "The media has been giving me a lot of heat lately but nothing compared to tent city! You think it's hot? It's 128 degrees there today!" The rain in Houston turned the streets and highways into rivers. The hurricane prompted the president to tweet: "Wow!" The cameras focused on him.

MB:
Good News

It's "a good news story." said the Homeland Security Chief, reporting the White House response to the devastation to Puerto Rico from Hurricane Maria. Responded the mayor of San Juan, "This is not a good news story." This is a people-are-dying story. I think of my friend Frank applying, in better days for Puerto Rico, to manage a ceramics factory in San Juan. When the interviewer asked, "Can you speak Spanish," Frank, who did not, said, "Si, Señor," after which he lingered on benches in Central Park to learn Spanish by ear. Arriving on the island, he found that the Puerto Ricans talked to everyone they met. That a stranger would say, "Come home, we'll kill a chicken and eat and talk." The good news was coconut corn starch pudding, yellow rice and pigeon peas with roasted pork. The good news was the Puerto Rican hibiscus, the good news was the spice. adobo, the good news was work. One night janitor Joe took Frank on an *assalto* in the mountains. where guitarists sang beneath a window. The homeowner rose to invite them in, and to put out rum and food, but something larger was in store, which began when each person sang a rhyming verse about the host, though Frank's Spanish was too weak, and he did not sing. Ah, but the Puerto Ricans believed that a non-singer must be suffering. The guitarists then played "Home on the Range" so that he could. The plant keys jingling in his pocket became the rhythm section. Then the host led them to the house next door to begin again, and so on and so forth to seven houses, more rum and the singing louder. Each host in turn to be honored with a full round of musical salutes. It may be true in this most divisive of times that whoever cannot sing is suffering the more. We must hope that our citizenry is able to tell good news from bad news, action from inaction, and a finger from a helping hand.

CM:
Fake News

The radio program on fake news featured writers from Algiers and Almaty, exiles from Gaza and Mogadishu, and a professor of journalism, who mourned the decline of his profession—which he blamed on a changing economy, the rise of social media, and the ignorance of élite journalists who distance themselves from the concerns of ordinary people. When it was my turn to speak about the hazards of reporting on the Balkan Wars, I remembered shivering uncontrollably in an unheated bus stalled on a snowy mountain road in Macedonia; a filmmaker's decision to portray Croatia as a proto-fascist state before he had even visited the country; and waking before dawn in Sarajevo to the sound of artillery. I learned to head for the other side of a conflict when I heard myself parroting the arguments of those I had interviewed—and still I missed the meaning of what I was reporting on: how the horrors spawned by the death of one political order were just the beginning of a story left untold. How hard it is to see what is right before our eyes. Fake news, for example, which we did not recognize to be the continuation of politics by other means until it was too late. The writers and exiles, skilled as they were at discriminating between fact and fiction in the tragedies defining the histories of their homelands, did not dare to interrupt anyone.

MB:
Saul

My father, Saul Bell, was not Saul Bell. The gatekeeper at Ellis Island could neither hear, nor respect, a Ukrainian surname up from steerage. Perhaps it sounded to him like gargling. Hence, he told my father, "You are now Saul Bell." repeating the name of someone ahead in the line. After that, there are knots in the family tree. His older brother married my mother's older sister. Harry, the brother, had taken the name "Cardon." I might have been, therefore, Marvin Botsian, which is as close as I can come to the original family name. Nor did we know my father's birthday, there being no documents. Nor would he tell us more than a few Old World stories, not even the details of his escape. Home from a day's work in the five-and-ten, he read the *New York Daily News*. Long after his early death, I returned annually for twenty years to eastern Long Island for two winter months. It was not my intention to feel at home, but the resonance of the commonplace reminded me of the daily lives about which I was, in youth, oblivious. In the film *Diner*, I recognize the characters and events from that time, when a diner was the last stop after every nighttime occasion, and always at the register stacks of the *Daily News* and the *New York Post*. The investigative, even accusatory, tone of the *Daily News*, the brief bursts of city news, the knife-in-the-gut headlines, and a little national coverage of the scandalous were plenty to go with the comics. The five-and-ten wasn't selling $500 purses and $800 shoes, and neither was the *News*. The daily tabloid was awash in the bold type of raw energy. We knew our place, a community without irony or nuance, and had a natural belief that what we cared to know didn't take long to report. Later, we subscribed to the larger-size *Herald Tribune*, though I don't recall ever seeing it lying around opened.

CM:
Lyall

My middle name, a Scottish surname derived from the Old Norse word for wolf, came from my father's father; my family's frugality I trace to our Lyall forebears, who comprise a sept of Clan Sinclair in the Scottish highlands. My grandmother, for example, would dry paper towels on the toaster for reuse and mash potatoes with sour milk, while my grandfather, a devout fisherman, grieved over losing a hand-tied fly to a trout that swallowed the hook. One day in the spring of my thirteenth year he took me fishing on a stream that ran through Jackie Kennedy's estate—which hardly impressed me. Bored, I contrived to fall into the cold water, which filled my waders, obliging him to drive me home. He knew what I had done—AT&T's retired director of personnel was a good judge of character—and yet he did not dispute my claim of having slipped on a rock. This was to be our last outing—he was dead before the dog days of summer; my subterfuge haunts me still. Perhaps you have seen the film detailing how the wolves reintroduced into Yellowstone National Park transformed the landscape? Fearing the predators, deer began to avoid the rivers, which changed course as plants regenerated along their banks; rabbits, weasels, and foxes thrived; songbirds returned, restoring the natural order. For Easter my grandfather gave me three shares of AT&T stock, which reverted to cash when the company was broken up. Mary, Queen of Scots, hunted wolves in the forests of Atholl, where my people came from. They wolf-proofed their coffins with flagstones. What we inherit matters less than the force and direction of the wind.

MB:
Rim Trail, Los Alamos

It happened at Bandelier National Monument where on a previous visit we had lingered inside the resonant chambers of Anasazi caves. On this morning, we walked a narrow rim trail to a sharp turn facing a waterfall. We had reversed course when two large dogs emerged from around a bend, racing toward us. The leaders of a wild pack, I feared, as I looked for anything that might be used in defense. Then I saw that there were only two—not dogs, but fully grown wolves. Were they ever going to see or smell us? Closing on us, they lifted their heads and left the trail, separating left and right, downhill then up to the tops of hills to either side, each immobile to observe us. After a while, the female walked off, while the male stayed on to make sure about us. Dorothy said, then, "You know, you can't tell anyone about this. They won't believe you." Moreover, the official position, as a park ranger insisted (after asking where I was from) was that there were no wolves in New Mexico, only coyotes. Well, I had seen plenty of coyotes, and I knew from you that wolves were being quietly reintroduced into national parks. These two must have just been set free, running as they were on a trail used by humans. A month later, we stopped at Wolfhaven in Tenino, Washington, where a visiting group had been registering nighttime wolf howls in the Cascades. Standing next to the program director, I reminded him that "There are no wolves in New Mexico," before asking what I'd seen. "I think you saw wolves," he said, with what I remember as a knowing twinkle. I suppose that, had I made all this up, it would be the lie that tells the truth. It's because it is true that, as Dorothy said, no one will believe me.

CM:
Stained Glass

I may have invited the wolves into the den, she said, reflecting on her decision to expand the board of her literary nonprofit, which was in dire need of funds. The new members, a best-selling writing couple, brought to the table money and money-making ideas at odds with her mission, which was to marry writing to the preservation of the wild—the subject of her own work, in film and on the page. Her true calling she discovered after a long career in stained glass, apprenticing at a workshop in Aspen and then accepting commissions from around the world. But she never mentioned her artisanal past when we met in the desert, where over shots of tequila she praised the horses on the ranch to which she made periodic retreats, or when we hiked in the Rockies. One day on the trail to Maroon Bells she identified the camp robber circling me as a Steller's jay—one of nine species named after the eighteenth-century German naturalist, the majority of which were either endangered or extinct. How she celebrated the bird alighting on my hand—and how I wish that when her cancer returned I had been a better friend. We fell out of touch when she left the nonprofit, which is to say: she could no longer help me. And what the light refracting through my window this morning reveals is what I did not wish to see, then or now: the wolf was me.

MB:
The Tally

Along with my Tom Mix decoder badge had come a small booklet showing the many places on his body Tom Mix had been injured. He had done most of it to himself, stunts for his movies. The chart covered broken bones, ruptured joints and torn tendons, but not heartaches or regrets. Nor errors of commission or omission. When Dorothy's mother was dying in southern Illinois, no one would give up a plane seat for Dorothy to get there in time. Without someone to blame, the event rests in between what someone could have done and what they failed to do. If I look back, I wonder what my father and I would have talked about had he lived longer. Would-haves and should-haves? We were not given to analysis, least of all self-analysis. Our era was an Age of "None of Your Business" and "Suck It Up." Young men who erred were not sent to jail but to the military. Most crimes were handled off the books. Good deeds were done in private, no one need know. How, in the welter of years, can one "be there" for everyone for whom one has felt affection? My list of friends and good acquaintances who have passed away is nearing two hundred. I still know them. I liked one, I helped one, I failed one—take your pick. Only the wholly selfish have no regrets. A tally of our errors is fodder for biographers, but I remain more amazed at how much goes right. My favorite cartoon is of a man in an easy chair holding a newspaper open to the obits on which the individual headlines read, TWENTY YEARS YOUNGER THAN YOU… FIFTEEN YEARS YOUNGER THAN YOU… THIRTY YEARS YOUNGER THAN YOU. *Carpe diem* means not looking back. But we do.

CM:
Drought

The dry riverbed in Isfahan in 2009 was for me the first sign of the drought that continues to afflict Iran. There were paddleboats lined up in the sand, women in black chadors crossing the river on foot, as if it were a desert wash, men on benches arguing over when the Zayanderud (Life Giver) stopped flowing into the city or if the sixteenth-century Bridge of Thirty-Three Arches, Si-o-se Pol, an architectural wonder of the Safavid dynasty, was in danger of crumbling. Lake Urmia, once the largest saltwater lake in the Middle East, had shrunk by ninety percent, spawning dust storms; hydrologists said the draining aquifers could not sustain Iran's population, which the Supreme Leader wanted to double. The tally of bad decisions—rampant dam construction, subsidies for farmers to plant thirsty crops like wheat, water diverted for political reasons—inspired protests, auguring, perhaps, the downfall of the clerical regime. Persians have long known the glories of empire—the Safavid shahs ruled one of the Gunpowder Empires, which extended from Bahrain and Iraq eastward into Afghanistan—as well as the costs in terms of death, destruction, and the loss of territory, natural resources, and prestige. No wonder the mullahs blamed the protests on the Great Satan, who in one disguise or another is always lurking near the porticoes of a bridge that may collapse at any time. For God's sake, give the thirsty man a drink!

MB:
Speaking in Tongues

Near the dead end of Senix Creek a narrow inlet that came from the Great South Bay to within a block of Main Street, the congregation we called "Holy Rollers" met to be possessed. We gave their small clapboard church a wide berth as we passed, thinking the glossolalia an affliction. If it was of the Holy Spirit, well, it was insufficiently melodious for our young ears, as was the tormented pitch of the cantor at the synagogue. Off the rickety, wooden walkway at water's edge floated the doctor's cabin cruiser in the town's only boathouse. Here's the thing: in a small world like ours, every decision was solely of the moment. The air was clear, the waterways full and the soil fertile with worms. If change were to occur to our climate, if the salt waters were to be polluted, if the air should become impure and the sky foreboding, it would be fate, no one to blame. We knew little of the sciences other than they would feed, shelter and heal the world. The Great Satan? America was the home of Democratic Optimism. Little was said about slaves or Native Americans. Driving on the bridges connecting our island to the city, we pointed to the skyline, admiringly.

CM:
Proportion

My father's refrain—*dead as a doornail*—came back to me at the door to the Serbian monastery of Hilandar, on the Holy Mountain of Athos, in Greece. The expression may have originated in the medieval practice of hammering a large-headed stud known as a doornail and then bending or clinching it to secure it. Langland used it in his allegorical poem *Piers Plowman*: "Faith without works is feebler than nothing, and dead as a doornail." And my father applied it to anything he did not like: unions, teachers, Democrats. The carpenter who built our house fired an apprentice for failing, twice in one morning, to clinch a ceiling nail. He told me that what he valued most in the construction of a door was its size in proportion to the rest of the façade— an idea that haunted me at the age of thirteen, because it suggested a form of knowledge available only to those accepted into the guild, which had cast out the apprentice. The guest master at Hilandar refused to let me stay for the night, claiming there was no room—which seemed unlikely in the dead of winter. No doubt he harbored ill will toward all Americans in the wake of the NATO air campaign against Serbian forces in Kosovo, and as I hiked in the dark toward the next monastery, which was reputed to be especially wary of foreign pilgrims like me, I feared the worst—which, as it turned out, was not sleeping in a forest populated by wolves but everything that followed.

MB:
Fate

Our plane could not return to Oahu, where a storm had come up, nor could it go on to Maui, where it was due, but where now there was also a storm. As we bounced in the air between islands, hoping to outlast one of the two storms, the woman seated ahead of me pulled the call button. The stewardess fought her way forward, grabbing seat backs from row to row, to ask what was needed. "My daughter," said the woman, motioning toward the person in the window seat, "wants to know if we are going to die." The stewardess replied that what we were experiencing was common, was normal, was routine, which did not answer the question. Maybe she was thinking, "Why ask," indifferent to the air pockets that kick plates and glasses to the ceiling, inured to hard landings and to the lurch of braking after coming in hot on a short strip. Long past her apprenticeship, any concerns she still had were tempered by the camaraderie of colleagues and the humor in a gate agent offering meal coupons to the nauseated—a pro unconcerned that a traffic controller's screen looks like a sky with no space. We who feel the nerves of air travel can no longer imagine the bareback horse rides the luckier peasants endured to escape the Czar, or feel the treks of this time's Syrians hoping for safe exile from the shrapnel of a broken world. All day and every day, we overfly life and death. The distances we cover in a wink take us up and away. We board on autopilot. Aloft, we lean back as if out of the world. It was Dickens, starting his *Christmas Carol*, who wrote, "Old Marley was as dead as a door nail." We live fated. The monk who turned you away was asleep at the wheel. Every landing needs a hero. Sometimes the passengers applaud.

CM:
Autopilot

A night of journalists swapping war stories at the bar: so many close calls in Bosnia, Chechnya, Afghanistan, Iraq, Congo. . . One hitched a ride on a cargo plane in Central Africa—a short hop expected to last less than ninety minutes—and when the flight entered its third hour he knew something was wrong. A tap on the door to the cockpit yielded no reply, so he pushed it open to find both pilots sound asleep, with newspapers spread across their faces to block out the sun. *Thank God for autopilot*, he said. So much depends upon the smooth clicking of the gears: one thing, and then another, and then, perhaps, catastrophe. Have I gone through life on autopilot? I took a humanitarian flight to the besieged capital of Sarajevo—an Ilyushin II-76 that corkscrewed toward the runway for an assault landing and then, just before touching down, rose abruptly. *We are returning to Zagreb,* the Russian pilot said over the intercom. *There is shooting at the airport.* You never hear the bullet that kills you. After we landed in the Croatian capital, the wingman examined the fuselage, which was riddled with bullet holes. One summer in Raleigh I worked for a carpenter, who said with a straight face that WD-40 could solve any problem. He would order me to move a fencepost or adjust my sightline *right much*. How much was *right much*? I could not say.

When

MB:
Doneness

May 29, 1919. Stillwater, Minnesota. Charles Strite, unhappy with the burnt cafeteria toast at his workplace, files a patent for the first pop-up toaster. The mass brutality of the recently concluded First World War did not fore-tell high-tech warfare at a distance. We were yet to experience exponential change. Hence, a small convenience could brighten the mornings before work and school. In the time it took to toast two slices of the mealy American bread at which Henry Miller poked fun, my father drank four glasses of hot water, an Old World digestive cleanser. Dinner times, however, we chewed a dense pumpernickel, which needed no such curing. I think now it was, in my father's mind, a vestige of his rural Ukraine. It's a pure nostalgia that attends a gadget that needs but a lever, a spring and a dial to lend the first meal of the day a little pop. The new pop-up toasting was fun. The cliché advice to build a better mousetrap was wrong. Build a better toaster and the world will beat a path to your door and to the bank that gives them free to new account holders. "You do not have to watch it," crowed the ad for Strite's better toaster. From gadgets like the pop-up toaster to the flying autopilot and the self-driving car, civilization has been a brilliant holding action against doom. We used to ask for seconds just to use the new toaster.

CM:
Tall Ships

July 4TH, 1976. From the rooftop of an apartment building in lower Manhattan I watched the regatta of tall ships sailing into New York Harbor for the bicentennial celebration of the Declaration of Independence. *Hair of the dog*, said a friend, pouring mimosas. The water glinting in the morning sunlight made my head pound; the sight of the white sails and rigging left me yearning for the sea, perhaps because I was reading Joseph Conrad. Navies from around the world were represented in the Parade of Ships, including a pair of German barques surrendered to the Soviet Union in 1946 as war reparations. Even then I knew I would not go to sea, confirming Conrad's insight: *Love and regret go hand in hand in this world of changes swifter than the shifting of the clouds reflected in the mirror of the sea.* By nightfall I was drunk again, driving south toward the fireworks emporia and my job at the lumberyard; when I drifted into the median on the interstate, falling asleep to the music of the Beatles ("While My Guitar Gently Weeps"), a trucker following me flashed his high beams on and off until I woke. This ringing in my ears might be the sound of the rigging the lookout registered on his last morning at sea, when the sky was red.

MB:
The Rollaboard

1987, Northwest Airlines pilot Robert Plath invents the rollaboard, to be patented in 1989. Its two wheels and long handle are the future, though men must first get past the idea that using the wheels undermines their macho mien. Change is tricky at any time because we are predisposed to believe that what is now is normal. Even an ocean crossing in steerage must have seemed to emigres a lucky break. It is but one of the many things about which I neglected to ask my father. In an age of exponential change, travel too has been transfigured. Travelers, porters and bellhops had to be happy about luggage wheels. Still, Plath was thought a tinkerer, no Einstein, no Curie. It's thirty years before his brainchild, and I'm lugging a suitcase I can barely lift through Grand Central Station on my way to Fort Bragg, North Carolina. A young man offers to help and I let him, too naïve to understand that he intends to make off with it. Of course, he drops it after four steps and runs off. Do I think that someday luggage will have wheels? No. Do I think that someday working ships, once vessels of privation, terror, hardtack and scurvy, will be followed by pleasure boats and cruise liners, and that the tallest ships will be seen as magically windswept? I am unable to foresee beyond whatever it is I am to do next. Will someday an automobile wake up a dozing driver on its own? They say it's coming. For me it took NoDoz, the "fast acting keep alert tablets," the car windows rolled down, the heater off, the fan turned up, and the radio at blast. Can I drive the 400 miles home from college on snow while tapping my foot? Half naïve and half stupid, but young, I am immortal, and I need no help.

CM:
Normalization

Czechoslovakia, 1969-1987. *Czech humor*, said the guide, translating the directions to Wenceslas Square, scrawled in Russian on the side of a building, that once lured Soviet tanks into a dead-end. How to erase vestiges of the "Prague Spring"—the loosening of restrictions, the opening of a space for civic dialogue? A half million Warsaw Pact troops invaded Czechoslovakia, reformers were jailed, and with the signing of the Moscow Protocol the Party reestablished control, spreading fear through what came to be known as *Normalization*, a word that first appeared in the 1848 translation of a German book titled *Errors of Physicians in the Practice of Water-cures*. Scientists originally used the term to describe a return to normalcy in the natural order or the human body; it acquired a political dimension in 1937, when *The Times* highlighted "the normalization of Polish-German relations." Pundits invoke it now to describe how unacceptable behavior—an American president lying with impunity—becomes acceptable: a process designed to create a state of affairs hitherto unimaginable except, perhaps, to the authors of political drama. *The worst thing*, the playwright-turned-president Václav Havel argued in his 1990 New Year's address to his newly independent nation, *is that we live in a contaminated moral environment*. He assumed his countrymen had not proposed him for this position to lie to them like his predecessors. He pledged to practice the art of the impossible—improving ourselves and the world. I could vote for that.

MB:
Tact

1816, invention of the stethoscope by René Laennec at the Necker-Enfants Malades Hospital in Paris. A contrivance borne of Dr. Laennec's discomfort at placing his ear on a woman's chest to hear her heart. The good doctor's wooden, monaural tube would be followed by the stethophone and the acoustic, electronic, fetal and doppler stethoscopes. This perfection of an outside-the-body ear, descended as it was from one physician's temperament, represented a now fading impulse toward tact. What lies between submission and rebellion? Could not moving to Canada to avoid fighting the Vietnam war be seen as a form of tact? Considering, like they say, the alternative, is not civil disobedience a form of tact? It is tact if it sheathes a dagger. It is not tact if it pokes the rain cloud. It is tact if it shades your eyes. It is not tact if it turns up the heat. It is tact if it scuffs its shoes. It is not tact if it stomps on your foot. Is there a civil way forward between submission and rebellion? I think of the Olympic gold medalist wrestler who, his daughter's first date having arrived to pass muster, came out of the kitchen bearing an axe. Now *that's* tact.

CM:
Short Program

19 July 2018. My younger daughter and I were touring the Julliard School when the news broke that Denis Ten, Kazakhstan's first Olympic medalist in figure skating, had been murdered in an attempted carjacking in Almaty. Ten belonged to the Korean minority in his country, the last Soviet republic to gain independence, and since I have a passing interest in the history of Koreans in Russia—their migration to the Far East, their indigenization under the Soviets, their deportation to Central Asia—I began to follow him after the Sochi Olympics in 2014, where he won the bronze medal, cheered on by his fellow Russian speakers. In a video for the 2018 Games in Pyeong-chang, South Korea, which Ten viewed as a kind of homecoming, his great-great-grandfather having won military fame fighting for Korean independence from Japan, he described his development into a world-class skater—the discipline, the disappointments—in the same artistic terms as our guide at Julliard, a composition student who played in a rock band. My daughter was thrilled. *No one knows what's behind the curtain,* Ten said in the video. *On the ice we are all equal.* It is believed that apples originated in Almaty, which means Father of Apples, and the trees were leafing out when I visited this spring. On my last day I went for a hike in the nearby mountains, where I saw an outdoor skating rink more than a mile above sea level. The thieves sought the mirrors on Ten's car, which were worth $86. A Canadian chore-ographer was about to start working with him on his new short program. My daughter thinks it is almost impossible to get into Julliard.

MB:
Iceberg

April 15, 1912. The eight musicians hired to entertain on the Titanic played as one to calm the passengers pressing to board lifeboats as the ship slid lower. Although surely there was some savage behavior among the desperate, the players still hoped to soothe the ill-fated passengers. Survivors would say later that the musicians played, at the last, "Nearer, My God, to Thee," though it was in fact the crew and passengers of the SS Valencia who sang it as they sank off the Canadian coast in 1906. Will the Titanic be the metaphor for democracy, swamped by a surge of lies, greed and treason? The ship took two hours and forty minutes to sink, as did the scenes set in the past in the wildly profitable movie based on the tragedy. I saw the film in a row of film-buff friends who, it turned out, were each sneaking peeks at their watches, as was I. Unsurprisingly, the film won the Oscar for Best Picture in 1998. Bamboozle, thy name is art. A look back is not a look ahead. It is 2018, and the glaciers are melting.

CM:
The Place of the Green Wand

Yasnaya Polyana, November 20, 1910. Tolstoy and his brother believed that in the woods of their estate there was a green wand inscribed with the secrets of happiness and immortality. I like to think that in the hours before the novelist died, at the train station in Astapovo, he had an inkling that *War and Peace* and *Anna Karenina* might live forever—though he had long repudiated the books that brought him global fame. His flight from his family, wealth, and acclaim was rash, and yet when I stood before his grave, a mounded rectangle of green at the edge of a clearing, I understood his yearning to be free of it all. News was breaking in America that a fiction writer I regarded as an older brother had resigned his professorship in disgrace, after the revelation of an illicit affair with a minor. Once at a party I heard him tell two students flirting with him that he was just a catch and release kind of guy, which I believed even as evidence accumulated to the contrary. Tolstoy signed away the copyright to his books and the deed to his lands before he boarded a train with no particular destination in mind, imagining he would never return to Yasnaya Polyana—where he was lying in repose when German soldiers commandeered his house in World War II and turned it into a hospital, burying their dead around him in the Place of the Green Wand. For we are all equal in death. Mute painters were holding an exhibit outside his house on the day I visited. They gestured wildly to one another, their joyful silence extending into eternity.

MB:
Mistake Out

Invention of the Post-it, 1974. Diminutive reminders that could not be weap-
onized, but might mark the stages of a novel or editorial. Church choir
member Arthur Frye, remembering a reusable adhesive created accidentally
six years earlier by a 3M colleague, makes stick-on bookmarks for his hymnal.
Post-its will become ubiquitous, unlike Bette Nesmith Graham's "Mistake
Out," later to be known as "Liquid Paper," for which she received a patent
in 1958. Until "Mistake Out," a single typo meant starting over. Technology
overtook "Liquid Paper" but not Post-its, perhaps because using small Post-
its feels like a game, while "Liquid Paper" was our inner schoolmarm. *The
New York Times* has published in September of 2018, an op-ed. whose anony-
mous author reports that Trump personnel are surreptitiously practicing
what could be called "Mistake Out." Nonetheless, this is the Age of Post-
its, which can be many times relocated, and thus they help us to put things
off.

CM:
Erasure

Invention of Liquid Paper, 1956. The Embassy in La Paz provided our delegation with an oxygen tank to ward off altitude sickness, which we drained in no time, and on a walking tour of the city the local staff encouraged us to drink tea brewed with cocoa leaves, which did nothing for my headache. Of our visit to the Basilica of San Francisco I recall only that the original structure, a straw-and-adobe convent built in the mid-sixteenth century, collapsed after a heavy snowfall. Nor do I remember the text we chose for the seminar, which was the centerpiece of our mission. Etched vividly in my memory, however, was our control officer's consternation when we asked her to buy correction fluid for a writing exercise in erasure. The classroom was on the fifth floor of a high-rise without a working elevator; on each landing, when we stopped to catch our breath, I marked the progress of the setting sun. Fernando Pessoa's maxim—*Everything stated or expressed by man is a note in the margin of an erased text*—was the starting point for a discussion on the idea of erasure—of peoples, places, and languages—and then we led the students through several iterations of an exercise, instructing them to white-out words, phrases, and sentences, their pages turning whiter and whiter until no more than a dozen words remained, each signifying a different turning of the imagination, none more ruthless or despairing, or so I thought, than what informed my journal entry later that night. I could barely breathe.

MB:
Past Present

1876, the first crematorium in North America is built in Washington, Pennsylvania. Mine is for later. This morning, out the window of Caribou Coffee, a long stripe of a train is passing, headed by three locomotives, while I linger to drain my to-go cup. For me, coffee shops have long borne an air of story and thought. Yesterday, among the retirees at Caffè Crema the one we call "the bear man," who travels to take close-up photos of bears, with no intention of selling them, tells me of an Alaskan glass blower who houses the ashes of the cremated in glass sculptures. For a man whose mother had so wanted to travel but never could, the glass man made marbles containing her ashes. Taking the marbles and a slingshot, the son traveled to places his mother had wanted to see and slingshot a marble into each. One went into the Colosseum in Rome. Another onto an arctic beach where penguins gather to guard their young. Can one change the past by thinking about it? In the coffee houses, they say no. We used to sound our car horns whenever we were driving parallel to a moving train. Sometimes, we got a reply. Being a grownup means knowing that things end. Slowly the rails go down and under.

CM:
Grizzly Man

Werner Herzog, 2005. The panel on environmental writing included Timothy Treadwell, who was garnering attention for his first book, *Among Grizzlies: Living with Wild Bears in Alaska*. After a heroin overdose, he developed a close relationship with grizzlies, claiming to gain their trust, and when the panel wrapped up another writer said, *He's going to get himself killed.* I knew something about taking chances for the sake of a story, even if my taste for adventure had diminished with the birth of our first child. Hannah arrived near the end of the war in Bosnia, and when I returned from my last reporting trip to Sarajevo, which coincided with the signing of the Dayton Accords, I had pages of notes on the Serbian exodus from the city and a case of double pneumonia. What I failed to record at the time was the ferocity with which Lisa kept Hannah away from me until I stopped coughing, marking a shift in our relations that shaped my experience of watching Herzog's documentary about a man whose obsession and willful ignorance doomed him and his girlfriend to be mauled by a grizzly; only his watch survived, which is probably still ticking.

MB:
Medical

September 28, 1928, the discovery of penicillin by Scottish doctor Alexander Fleming. It grew "naturally," and naturally no one paid much attention. Years went by before the doctors realized what they had. It was different for vaccines, but now comes the anti-vaccine movement, which prefers contagion to inoculation. It remains true that there is only so much that medicine and surgery can do. When this past summer I arrived at the bedside of my sister Ruby, who was unable to move in the bed, resistant to the foam swabs with which the nurse wet her lips, her tongue too thick to allow her to speak, I leaned down to her and she forced herself to whisper "I want to die." We sometimes forget that life-giving medications and treatments are holding actions, just as a smarter Timothy Treadwell might have known that a dialogue with grizzlies is a high-wire act from which the performer must ultimately fall. I was an Army officer when our son took ill where we lived off-base in a town called (absent irony) Fortville. We met the doctor at a storefront office, where he left his car running—it was a cold winter—and opened the office to take a listen through his stethoscope. It was nighttime. "He has scarlet fever," he said. "No, he doesn't have scarlet fever," we told him. He reconsidered and said, "He has diphtheria." "No," we said, "he doesn't have diphtheria." Our son had a high fever, for which the doctor suggested we take him out in the snow. In fact, he was coming down with the measles. Antibiotics, vaccines, medical guesswork, holding actions and hospice—the body, ramshackle or treasure, is also a plaything.

CM:
The Werther Effect

The Sorrows of Young Werther, Johann Wolfgang von Goethe, 1774. Theorists of social contagion trace the idea that harmful social influences can be transmitted like infectious diseases to the rash of suicides that followed the publication of Goethe's semiautobiographical novel. Like his doomed protagonist, melancholy young men wore blue coats and yellow trousers to shoot themselves or jump from bridges—stylized statements that convinced some European authorities to ban the book. Goethe composed a poem for the second edition, admonishing readers not to follow his example. Two hundred years passed before a sociologist coined a term for a form of contagion—the Werther effect—that soon infected my hometown. Keith's younger brother took his life, and others followed suit, as others always do. Consider the Buddhist monk who set himself on fire at an intersection in Saigon to protest the war, inspiring other self-immolators, including a fruit-seller in Tunis who sparked the Arab Spring. Then remember the suicide bombers in London, Madrid, and Manchester; the killers stalking houses of worship in Charleston, Pittsburgh, and Christchurch; the white supremacists chanting *Blood and Soil* in Charlottesville, MAGA-hatted men and women threatening journalists at Trump rallies, online trolls desperate to own the libs. Some take their marching orders from what they read, see on TV, or track on social media, inoculating themselves, or so they think, against the viruses circling the globe. Think again.

MB:

April Fools' + 1

April 2, 2019, U.S. President Donald Trump declares that wind turbines cause cancer. The comedians snicker, and we guffaw. Think back to the Piels beer television ads of *1955* to *1960* in which the comics Bob Elliott and Ray Goulding voiced the animated characters Bert and Harry marketing Piels. The ads were meant to focus attention on the brand, but Bert and Harry sometimes entertained us as if they were still getting around to it. Was it the cartoon Bert or the cartoon Harry who sent the other for a table and was told to stall by doing bird calls, which he did until the table appeared, by which time it was too late. Trump is an unwitting practitioner of the method: to entertain us until it is too late. Viewers enjoyed the Bob and Ray ads but forgot for what product, and Piels resorted to the hard sell in which a song kept repeating "Piels, Piels, wonderful Piels" over pictures of people having fun. Schlitz, Pabst and Budweiser steamrolled the national beer world. January 6, 2018, Trump says "I'm a very stable genius." Are we having fun yet?

CM:
Tongue-Tied

June 6, 2019, Normandy Beach, France. The ceremony commemorating the 75th anniversary of the D-Day invasion of Normandy was delayed, according to U.S. President Donald Trump, by the interview he taped with FOX News—a mixture of grievance, insult, and deceit, with the American cemetery in the background. I was ruing, once again, the loss of the journals my father's godfather had kept during his medical service aboard the hospital ship USS Hope, which had set sail across the Pacific not long after the liberation of Paris. His meticulous record of the final campaign against Japan, during which his ship evacuated and tended to the wounded and dying from the Battles of Corregidor, Okinawa, and other islands, disappeared when I moved west, along with my dream of bringing his voice to life in a novel. I feared him in my childhood, perhaps remembering in some vestigial way his decision at our kitchen table in my infancy to use a pair of scissors to snip the band of tissue connecting my tongue to the floor of my mouth. My malnourishment he blamed on the fact that I was tongue-tied, which relieved my mother, who traced his brutal methods to the USS Hope. I did not speak until I was nearly two. Sometimes it is best to hold your tongue.

MB:
Native Tongues

The Duke of Deception, Geoffrey Wolff, 1979. A book of revelations. To be moved to write for an occasion is a sure cure for the wordless. You and I were there in the Bread Loaf barn to hear the stuttering author who had barged through his fear of his first-ever public reading so that his children would hear, prior to the publication of his memoir, the truth of their father's father, whose life as a con man had been unknown by his son. I recall, too, the novelist who, as a student, lengthened every question with an unstoppable stutter but who did not stutter on stage. Both writers would vanquish their genetic constraints. There are other reasons for not speaking. I will never know if my father would have said anything much about his escape from Ukraine under a horse-drawn load of hay, or his horseback ride to Poland and the voyage in steerage to America. Had he lived longer, still I think he would not have told. Indeed, it seems that asking PTSD veterans to speak of the horrors of their wars abroad is not therapeutic but destructive, as they go through them again. The desensitization training of the military did not carry over for those whom Rusk, McNamara and Bundy sent to Vietnam, and for whom no treatment could loosen their tongues about the whole truth. Our friend Rocky tells me of his ninety-nine-year-old mother, her faculties intact, who asks of him that he tell those at her "service" to enunciate clearly. We are lucky who are given the words to say enough.

CM:
"One More Cup of Coffee" (#1 of The Corey Quartet)

Rolling Thunder Revue: A Bob Dylan Story by Martin Scorsese, 12 June 2019. In the documentary assembled from archival footage and interviews, Scarlet Rivera, the violinist for Dylan's return to touring in the fall of 1975, explains the origin of the image she created on stage: *Mr. Tambourine Man gives us the opportunity to be whoever we wish to be.* Which is, of course, what an editor can offer to a writer. The film cuts to the annual Romani pilgrimage for the veneration of their patron saint, Sara, in Saintes-Maries-de-la-Mer, in the south of France, which Dylan attended not long before the tour. The feast day happened to be his birthday, which made him feel as if he were going home, perhaps because his wife shared the saint's name. He listened to a guitarist play until dawn, then accepted a cup of coffee for the road—the inspiration for "One More Cup of Coffee," a song that came to him in a dream. Left unsaid in the film is that it is regarded as a commentary on his crumbling marriage, and when the camera focuses on the interaction between him and the violinist in performance a kind of dark energy lights up the stage. *It was like one battery charging another,* is how Rivera's driver describes the drama playing out between the artists and the audience—an exchange of energy integral to any creative enterprise, I thought, pausing the video to reflect on all the kindred spirits I have found in the pages of *The Georgia Review*, thanks to the vision of that one-man band, Stephen Corey. *The future already exists,* Rivera says as she boards the tour bus, which Dylan is driving. *It's just a matter of tuning yourself to it.*

MB:
"Strikes and Spares" (#2 of "The Corey Quartet")

I thought I had recorded Michelangelo Antonioni's 1966 *Blowup*, but the on-screen guide was erroneous. Happily, before the wrong film there came "Strikes and Spares," the Pete Smith black-and-white short about bowling. After some instruction, the focus shifted to Andy Veripapa, the Italian-born ambidextrous bowler from Brooklyn who did tricks that defied physics. And all of them on undoctored alleys. Think of rolling a ball that takes out the dreaded 7-10 split. That's a skill some have. If you were Veripapa, however, you could deliver a ball that curved to the left, then to the right, to roll between glass lamps on its way to the pins. You could with a single ball knock down three pins placed across three alleys. Was seeing believing? Veripapa rolls a ball left to right where it travels between the legs of a line of 1934 bathing beauties before it twists its way to a strike. Rolls a ball that curves to the left, curves to the right, curves back to the left. Are you kidding me? When Stephen Corey, who bowls, comes to Iowa City, we make our way to Colonial Lanes, where I find out that at eighty-one I can't even jog to the line, and I roll a bunch of gutter balls, while Stephen mows down the pins with an arm swing like old and a delivery that kisses the alley. He doesn't seem embarrassed to be bowling with a has-been. Peter De Vries gets credit for the original phrasing of what became, "Writing is easy, except for the paperwork." How many hours are there in a Stephen Corey day? Seeing is believing. He must drink a lot of coffee.

CM:
Film Studies (#3 of "The Corey Quartet")

Zabriskie Point, 1970. If seeing is believing, then poor eyesight might account for my waning faith in eternal things, if not for Paul's reminder that what is unseen is eternal. For example, when Michelangelo Antonioni visited an eroded area in Death Valley called Zabriskie Point, he said, "I want to see 20,000 hippies out there making love, as far as you can see." But the dreamlike orgy scene he shot in the desert includes only two hundred men and women, clothed and covered in sand, lolling on the hills above a dry wash. My own experience of Death Valley was a little different. When my mother and her best friend drove our two families to California, they decided to cross Death Valley at night, fearing our station wagon would overheat. They bought two canvas water bags, and later, when they pulled over in the dark to refill the radiator, I got out to stretch my legs. Waves of heat washed over me like a benediction until my mother warned me to beware of rattlesnakes. This was what I remembered watching the film's final scene, when the heroine imagines a house atop a cliff blowing up again and again—a figure, perhaps, for the creative process: things come together, seen and unseen, and the artist sets out on another journey. Fare well, Stephen Corey.

MB:

The Bugaboos of Perplexity (#4 of "The Corey Quartet")

At the conclusion of the film *Il Postino*, Pablo Neruda stands on the shore of the Italian island where he lived in exile, and where a nearly illiterate post-man, inspired by the great poet, was hoping to romance the town beauty with the seductions of verse. Neruda learns that the postman, having won the object of his love, and having been invited to read a poem at a protest, was killed there in the chaos of police brutality. The actor Philippe Noiret, looking quite like Neruda, stands at water's edge as the camera pulls back and back until the great poet is but a speck in a vast indifferent landscape. I waited for the director at the Seattle Film Fest to speak about the symbolism of the movie's closing imagery, the finality of it, the realism of it in the face of romantic aspiration, but he did not. The death, the very day after the movie was finished, of the actor Massimo Troisi, who postponed heart sur-gery to play the part of the bicycling postman—was it not another fist in the face of romance? Not that knowing has ever stopped us, who lift a glass in toast to say "Life is sweet." "Bittersweet" being the more accurate word, it is central to the life force to investigate what's what—and, as Stephen Corey once put it, "to embrace the bugaboos of perplexity." Thank you, Stephen.

CM:
Ghosts

Mickelsson's Ghosts, John Gardner, 1982. The reviews of Gardner's final novel were brutal—one critic likened it to "mountains and mountains of loose black coal, shifting and sliding but burning no fire and making no light"— and that summer at Bread Loaf some attributed his drunkenness to literary despair. He was late for his morning lecture, and when I found him in his room drinking with his fiancée and another writer he was in no mood to go to the Little Theater, where he delivered the shortest lecture anyone could remember. *If you're not writing political,* he said, *you're not writing.* Then he strummed his guitar for a minute or two before returning to his room to continue partying. I developed a theory about his fall from grace, which ended the next month, just before his wedding, when he drove his motorcycle off the road. He survived colon cancer, two divorces, and assorted literary controversies, including a plagiarism charge, only to find he could not rid himself of the ghost that called him to write, in one form or another: how at the age of eleven, driving a tractor on the family farm, he had accidently crushed his younger brother to death. From his books, his attempts to exorcise the nightmares and flashbacks he suffered until his dying day, I am learning that what I witnessed and experienced in Sarajevo will not leave me be.

MB:
Holograms

Sept. 27, 2019, Beverly Hills, California, the Saban Theater. Holograms of Roy Orbison and Buddy Holly take turns not being there. A reviewer, against his expectation, said, "It wasn't creepy," but admits his mind wandered after two numbers. A tribute show, the audience had come to see the artists perform. They cheered the first appearance of Hologram Orbison. They moved to the beat when Holly jumped about the stage. Were the holograms memory blocks—in either sense of the phrase? Or both at once? Holograms, ghosts, people in dreams, the fabricated characters of fantasy, echoes of times past, déjà vu—they show up unbidden, living in the resonant cavities of the brain yet seeming to arrive from afar. Staying in Frost's cabin in New Hampshire, when poets who had slept there previously said they had met a nightly ghost, I welcomed the ghost but, whether awake or asleep, neither saw nor heard anything. I kept the bedroom door open, not that it would have been a hinderance. Free of the ghostly, I tell stories about friends who have died because, after all, I still know them. In that way, but only in that way, I bring them to life. I remember the insomniac John Gardner writing through the night at a small table in a Bread Loaf hallway, and wonder now if it was a way to avoid his lost brother. Those who paid $25 apiece to be in the moment with Orbison and Holly were largely satisfied and appreciative, though the reviewer noted that some left early, as had Orbison and Holly.

CM:
Kissing Snakes

The Fishermen, Sculpture Garden, Petrozavodsk, Russia, 21 October 2019. My guide, a linguistics professor from the state university, had remained single for so long that when she invited her friends to a wedding celebration, at the lakefront restaurant where we were dining, they did not believe she would marry the Egyptian computer scientist she had met on holiday in Alexandria; hence they brought no gifts to their nuptials. After lunch, walking along the embankment, she rehearsed the nicknames locals had bestowed on the post-modernist sculptures commissioned and presented to Petrozavodsk by its sister cities—*Woman with Four Breasts*; a series of posts called *Dogs' Joy*; and *Kissing Snakes*, two tall columns twisting toward each other, each topped with a metallic serpentine shape. The monument to Peter the Great had been moved from the city center to make way for one to Lenin—which was not re-moved when the Soviet Union dissolved. We had no time to visit Lenin Square, also called "Round Square" (the English translation of круглая площадь), before my overnight train departed for Moscow. The other passenger in my compartment was attached to one of the security services, though I could not make out the pin affixed to the lapel of his leather jacket. Nor did he speak to me or turn a page of the book he was reading, which was thick enough to be *War and Peace*. Our encounter was as unlikely, and perhaps inev-itable, as my guide's marriage or the pair of wire mesh fishermen overlooking the lake, who would soon be coated with ice; they had no nicknames. After midnight, when I realized my bunkmate would read until morning, I took an Ambien and slept like a baby.

MB:
Smiles

Nov. 13, 2019, the public impeachment hearings of Donald Trump. My father having come to the U.S. from Ukraine as a teen, I should like beets and borscht, and the bitter herbs of the seder, but I do not. My culinary affiliation with his Old World consists of the likes of bagels, garlic and halvah, though one can hardly find a true bagel any longer, even on the lower East Side of New York to which those fleeing poverty and pogroms came. When I delivered my son to his sublet on his move to New York, before leaving I fixed the mailbox, bought a duplicate door key, and pointed to a nearby deli, telling him to ask for a "bagel with a schmear." He was too shy to say such a thing, but half a year later his girlfriend told me that he had gotten better about it. She explained that he had ordered a bagel and, when the waitress asked if he wanted "a schmear," he had said yes. Such a small thing, it still makes me smile. Even the inquiry to establish the President's crimes linked to Ukraine has its humorous side, given his continuous "I'm rubber and you're glue" fibs. In good times and bad, we take our joy and delight from actions of which we were a part, even when it falls to us only to know the news and to speak of the obvious. I'm not saying everything is peachy keen, but there's a reason to smile.

CM:
Fantasy World

November 20, 2019, the public impeachment hearings of Donald Trump. When Jennifer Williams, a Foreign Service officer detailed to the vice president's office, swore an oath to tell the truth, the whole truth, and nothing but the truth to the House Intelligence Committee, I thought I recognized her from a cultural diplomacy mission a decade ago. My control officer's instructions for my first engagement in Beirut were unnerving, given the travel warnings issued by the State Department for Lebanon: take a taxi to Fantasy World, a family-themed fun park in Dahiya, a largely Shi'a district and Hezbollah stronghold in south Beirut, then cross the road to the high school. A young diplomat (Ms. Williams, if memory serves) was waiting for me with her security detail. She was anxious to start, and stayed only long enough to introduce me to the class, reminding me before she left to take a taxi back to my hotel and send her the receipts. I do not remember ever feeling so alone. But the students, who were fluent in Arabic, English, and French, seemed to embrace my idea that translating poems and stories from one language to another could be part of their literary apprenticeship. And when they read aloud the writing exercise I gave them—describe a room in your house—it felt as if they had invited me into their lives. This was a fantasy, of course, like the fun park across the road, which belonged to Hezbollah's financier, or the belief that truth might prevail in Congress. The diplomat testified that Trump's phone call to the Ukrainian president was "unusual and inappropriate." It took me forever to hail a taxi in that part of town.

MB:
The Art of the Deal

1987, a book "by" Donald Trump, ghosted by Tony Schwartz. January 22, 2020, President Trump says, about the coronavirus pandemic, "We have it totally under control." Jan. 24, "It will all work out well." He explains that it will "just disappear." Previously, he called it "the Democrats' new hoax." March 24, 2020, over 53,000 people in the U.S. and territories have tested positive, and over 700 have died. Trump has caused a run on hydroxychloroquine, a drug needed for lupus and rheumatoid arthritis, falsely claiming it treats the virus. He refuses to invoke the power to pay companies to make ventilators with which to save the sick. Trump, who it seems has betrayed banks, stiffed workers, and stolen from charities, now shows the qualities of a wholesale serial killer. My wife and I, seniors with "underlying conditions," will be indoors for a long time, while Trump is eager to tell us not to self-isolate but to make the economy look better for his re-election campaign. Meanwhile, our son in NYC, a trained ninja, is buying things for us he thinks we should have. Our other son, who FaceTimes from Tennessee, convinced us to buy LifeStraws. They say you can stick one in the mud and suck up clean water. If only that applied to the Trump administration, devoutly lying, while "Let them eat cake" Melania, is having a tennis pavilion built on the White House lawn. Who will play tennis there? This time of "social distancing" is no time for Socratic dialogue, but we can seek a smile here or there, to wit: Dorothy, out walking, heard someone across the street say, as his friend approached him, "I've got a tape measure, and I'm not afraid to use it."

CM:
The Plague

26 March 2020. I was rereading Camus' novel when the United States became the epicenter of the coronavirus pandemic, with more confirmed cases than any country and a thousand deaths. One month after Trump's declaration that COVID-19 would disappear, "like a miracle," this public health emergency was for the president not what the French writer had described in his diary as "the redeeming plague." Camus set his story in the coastal Algerian city of Oran, which had a history of epidemics, and while the plague he describes in minute detail is often regarded as a metaphor for life in Vichy France, it is first and foremost a disease. Quarantine resembles military occupation, it is true; also Sarajevo during the siege, which was where I first read *The Plague*. A friend suggested that Trump was leading a death cult. *What's next?* an Episcopal priest asked me in an email. *Frogs and boils?* The ten plagues of Egypt, sent by God and recounted in the Book of Exodus, which include turning the water of the Nile to blood, a thunderstorm of hail and fire, and enough locusts to cover the face of the earth, convinced the Pharaoh to free the Israelites from slavery. The president's dereliction of duty will cost many lives. In despair I snuck out of the house at dusk to go for a run, and when I started down the hill above the marsh I heard a chorus of spring peepers calling to their mates. It sounded like sleigh bells.

MB:
Aesthetic Wobble #6

March 28, 2020. Can we vindicate our yearning for beauty during a pandemic? Is there a writer's hazmat suit? Beginning to write at 2:30 in the afternoon, I noted the count of 116,448 coronavirus cases in the U.S. and 1,943 deaths. When I quickly reloaded the page, I saw that someone else had passed. By 2:41 the death toll was 1,978. Now Trump wants people to die for the Dow. New York Governor Andrew Cuomo, during the pandemic the most presidential spokesperson in the country, having asked in vain for sufficient federal assistance while New Yorkers perished, now could not keep from calling Trump's plan to get people into the streets by Easter "not aspirational, but asinine." Trump has told his sycophantic veep, Mike Pence, not to telephone governors insufficiently "appreciative" of him. I am bent from concern for my son and daughter-in-law residing on the 26th floor of a Brooklyn high-rise. He reassures me: "We take the stairs down and up," he says. "Nobody takes the stairs in New York!" Taking a break from writing this at 4:00 p.m., the U.S. death count stands at 1,979. One minute later: 1,993. Trumpism is exponential.

CM:
The True Believer

March 29, 2020. On my mother's birthday, one month to the day after her death, I counted out the pills remaining in my supply of hydroxychloroquine, an antimalarial drug used in the treatment of rheumatoid arthritis, to gauge how long I might have before my immune system resumed its attack on my joints. A Trump tweet extolling its miraculous healing properties for sufferers of COVID-19 led to a shortage of the drug, with doctors prescribing it for themselves and their families, and so the pharmacy cannot refill my prescription. The president's faith in a single study, dismissed by virologists, unnerved public health professionals accustomed to making policy recommendations based on scientific evidence. And his followers' belief in the misinformation he offers daily about the pandemic, despite media fact-checking, called to mind *The True Believer*, Eric Hoffer's study of mass movements and fanaticism, which once helped me understand my mother's trust in Richard Nixon. The stevedore wrote his first book in longhand between shifts on the San Francisco docks, then sent his only copy to Harvard University Press; when asked what he would do if the editor lost his manuscript, he said he would just write it out again, because he had it memorized. *The true believer is everywhere on the march*, he wrote in 1951—and this is still the case. My mother died of dementia on Leap Day, the date of the first American death from COVID-19, and since I last checked this morning the plague has claimed 172 more lives, medical supplies are running dangerously low in New York City, and Trump is boasting on Twitter about the television ratings his press conferences garner. If and when this finally comes to an end I hope that what we have written here—and what we may yet write—will be at once original and true.

Volume III

Here & Now

Here

CM:
Ransoms

From Twitter I learn that the Welsh word for self-isolation, *hunan ynysu*, can be translated as self-islanding—a working definition of our new dispensation, which has its own nomenclature. Here in the Peninsula neighborhood, where we shelter in place, practicing social distancing to avoid contracting the novel coronavirus, I recall stories my late friend, the Welsh writer Leslie Norris, used to tell: how in one bleak period of his life he would look over the page he had typed each day, crumple it up, and drop it in the trash can. His wife, Kitty, would retrieve the page, read it, and return it to the trash can. Leslie relished the idea that in his elegy for Edward Thomas he misnamed the white star-shaped flowers growing on the hill above the poet's house, calling them ransoms instead of ramsoms, which merited a citation in the OED. Sometimes I wondered how they survived their last years in Provo, Utah, feted by the Mormons at BYU, though they did not belong to the Church of Latter-Day Saints, and now it comes to me: they made an island for themselves at the base of the Wasatch Mountains. I had the good luck to dine with them regularly, gathering stories, it seems, for our self-islanding. Medieval Welsh bards, Leslie told me more than once, wrote their deathbed poems when they were still healthy. No telling when the end is nigh.

MB:
Endings

I am especially fond of literary endings in which a poem stops but the poetry continues. Does that not apply to deathbed poems written early? It's an up-in-the-air presence, a sailing away, a wave of insinuation, neither an aura nor an omen because endless. We were leaving the Salt Lake City airport for a long drive south when I turned to the *Deseret News* journalist in the back seat and asked, "Where do Mormons think Heaven is?" "Do you really want to know?" he asked. "We've got five hours," I said. And it came to pass that he told me the ins-and-outs, the ups-and-downs, the then-and-now, even the story of the borrowed garment for a hot date. He told of a mission where they competed with Jehovah's Witnesses to see who could find the next graveyard. He said (was he joking?) they received a pound of chocolates for each male soul and a half-pound for each female. It was a happy drive, though two years later he would walk by me without speaking. Having once written an article that displeased his editors, he had been welcomed back. In the age of COVID-19, a doctrine by which the faithful stockpile for emergencies and tithe on principle, even as they seek converts, looks like a business plan for a pandemic. In a safer time, at the Mormon university in Hawai'i, down the road from the Polynesian Cultural Center, where the Samoans do the haka and the hula dancers sway languidly, the man assigned to deliver the prayer before my poetry reading declared his certainty the audience would leave the event feeling spiritually uplifted. I knew I was being told to watch my step. Afterward, I played basketball with some of the teachers, and then we went for ice cream. I don't know if the Mormons have yet baptized every branch of my Ukrainian family tree. Can they ever? That's a lot of blood and chocolate.

CM:
Inheritance

A whistleblower's complaint to the IRS detailing how the Church of Jesus Christ of Latter-day Saints had misled its members about investments in its charitable accounts brought to mind the last time I saw my father's Aunt Kay. She was visiting family in Orem, Utah, in May 1987, finalizing preparations for her move from a 5,000-acre mountain ranch near Carmel-by-the-Sea. Her husband, Dudley, chairman of National Airlines, had been dead for twenty-five years, and she explained that when a Mormon deacon offered her disabled son a job she took that as a sign to convert—a decision, my father said, that would have caused Dudley to turn over in his grave. Aunt Kay was nearly seventy when the Mormons sent her on a mission to Hawai'i. Over lunch she described her friendship with Robinson and Una Jeffers; also Clint Eastwood; when asked about the ranch, Aunt Kay said she had decided to donate it to the Church for a conference center—which apparently was not built. The whistleblower claimed the investment manager had set aside $100 billion for the Second Coming of Christ, some of which was used to bail out failing companies instead of helping those in need—which gives new meaning to Paul's command to *store up for yourselves treasure in heaven, where moth and rust do not destroy, and where thieves do not break in and steal.* The tithing of the faithful might be put to better use in a pandemic. Poor Aunt Kay gave up everything to enter the Celestial Kingdom.

MB:
Bad News

April-June, 1954, the Army-McCarthy hearings. They overlapped my gradu-
ation from high school. I was glued to the TV, oblivious to the local damage
inflicted by McCarthyism and the Red Scare, but I could tell Tail Gunner
Joe was bad news. I had won the American Legion annual speech contest by
relating the Constitution to daily life, including baseball. I had won because
they weren't going to give first place to my friend, the son of a physicist at
Brookhaven National Lab, who had spoken about McCarthyism. Anyone
could be a commie, how were we to tell? Scientists were suspect. People who
thought twice were suspect. Suspicion stayed on the level of gossip kept
from the children. At least that. Jump to June 1, 2020. The powder keg of
police brutality has brought us once again face-to-face with the systemic rac-
ism of our country. Trump's response is to stand in front of a church holding
a prop bible fished out of Ivanka's $1,500 purse. To let him amble across the
street for a photo-op, a peaceful assembly has been tear gassed. The Arch-
bishop labels Trump's stunt "baffling and reprehensible." The Bishop says
she is outraged. The Mayor defines Trump's blatant ill-use of the church as
"shameful." Even a senior White House official is reported to have said,
"I'm really honestly disgusted. I'm sick to my stomach." I wonder which
speech contest topics are now considered unpatriotic. The McCarthy-Army
hearings lasted thirty-six days, while the blacklist of alleged Communist
sympathizers lasted a decade. The popularity of lies is an unfathomable
curse. To depend on the Trump government for truth is whistling in the
graveyard.

CM:
"Stairway to Heaven"

I watched the Watergate hearings, in the summer of 1973, between the lessons I gave as an assistant teaching tennis pro at the club across the road from our house. In the woods by the clay courts was a hut with a black-and-white TV set, and I date the beginning of my political education to the Senate questioning of witnesses. It was true that Nixon's coverup was not nearly as important to me at sixteen as the prospect of getting high, which did not happen until my parents took my sisters on a vacation to Block Island. They hired my boss, a law student who had squandered a tennis scholarship from the University of Miami, to stay at our house, and one day after work I was lying on my bed, having just smoked a joint, blissfully listening to a recording of "Stairway to Heaven," when he suggested we return to the club to work on my backhand. What I remember is how time seemed to slow down on the court as I slid into each stroke, certain I had never hit the ball so cleanly, until he asked me what the hell was going on. I did not answer, because I did not want to lose my summer job; and so began my education in truth telling—which has taken on new urgency in the face of Donald Trump's rampant lying. *All that glitters is gold*, Trump may think, like the heroine of Led Zeppelin's song—the opening licks of which, the courts have ruled, were not stolen from another band, since musicians have used these same chords for hundreds of years. There is still time, according to the songwriters, for her to choose a different road. Trump, not so much.

MB:
CHAZ

June 13, 2020. Capitol Hill, Seattle, where in 1982 we lived in a neighborhood friendly to LGBTQ and the arts, but now increasingly gentrified, has become the Capitol Hill Autonomous Zone after police boarded up the East Side Police Station and moved out. Black Lives Matter and Defund the Police demonstrations have co-opted the area, where for now music, poetry and free food support the protestors. I recall my 2011 walk through the Occupy Wall Street premises in New York City, where a narrow maze of pathways held music, meditation, craft classes, meals and a free library. Police encircled it, blocking neither entry nor exit. I cannot say that it effected a slowdown in rampant capitalism. Working backward, I am reminded, also, of the Vermont communes of the sixties and seventies, whose shared goods and ethics made no dent in the greed that today characterizes the Trump family. Does anyone doubt that the States would have all the protective gowns, face masks and ventilators they need if Trump got a royalty for each one? About the financial iniquity overtaking a wealthier Capitol Hill, a *Seattle Times* writer called it "a classic showdown of jocks and prom queens versus freaks and geeks." These protests against systemic racism, lit by police brutality against people of color, are so much more. Threatened by Trump, Seattle Mayor Jenny Durkan told him to go back to his bunker. It is a compounding flaw that a government can print money but not equity. Some years ago, when I told my son that I thought our minorities would save us, he said no, it will be our young people. Could we both have been right? We are holding our breath.

CM:
Gohmert

In 2011, on a visit to Corregidor in the Philippines, I eavesdropped on a conversation between Texas Congressman Louie Gohmert, his wife, and the American tour guide who had shepherded our graduate creative writing workshop around the island. A student signaled me to join him at the table next to the lawmaker's, and what we overheard was astonishing. The guide cautioned the Gohmerts not to feed the wild monkeys, which prompted the lawmaker to say that President Obama reminded him of a monkey; in the company of foreign leaders, his wife added, *Obama always looked dumber than anybody*. It was dismaying to hear the guide agree with them: his detailed knowledge about this volcanic crater, whose name is derived from the Spanish verb to correct, and the pair of crucial battless waged there in World War II, had impressed us on our tour with him. At different gun emplacements he had described the Japanese invasion and then the Allied liberation of Corregidor, bloody sieges that cost nearly 9,000 men their lives; at the entrance to the Malinta Tunnel complex, which had served as Allied headquarters until the fall of the island, he retold the story of General Douglas MacArthur's escape to Australia and famous promise: "I shall return." Neither the student nor I spoke until the Gohmerts left the inn, and then he said, "Our Congress." I had forgotten his comment until it was reported that in spite of the pandemic Gohmert will not wear a mask on the House floor unless he contracts COVID-19—which inspired me to look up the Urban Dictionary definition of a gohmert: "Any stupid, foolish, or obtuse public official."

MB:
Opera

At the 1986 Adelaide Arts Festival, the writers were given tickets to the premiere of a long-anticipated opera based on Patrick White's novel, *Voss*. A mostly interior story, it draws from the life of Ludwig Leichhardt, who set out to explore Australia and disappeared in the Outback. The opera was lackluster, and as the curtain fell the audience hurried its applause but had to hesitate as the curtain rose again simply to show a teacher reading to her charges of the greatness of Voss. Finally, the curtain came down to stay. We in the balcony were working hard to keep the applause going for our friend, the librettist. The actors took their bows, the composer and the conductor took theirs, and then it was time for the writer, who emerged from stage right, took a few steps and decided in the flush of accomplishment to hop up onto the low platform on which the opera had finished. Alas, he missed and fell flat on his face, *splat!*, prone on the stage. The audience gasped. In retrospect, it was true opera: the best moment of your life is also the worst moment of your life. The next day, our friend the librettist had a car and driver. I stopped at the window to congratulate him on the premiere. "Did you see me fall?" he asked. I was tempted to say, "The *whole country* saw you fall," but I only said, "You got up quickly." It's July 4, 2020, and the tragedy of the Trump presidency is being played out at Mount Rushmore, where the lead actor rages against his betters. Like opera, it has violence and betrayal and a chorus of sycophants. The goal of the main character is to see a hotel in Russia bearing his name—hence, despite a heavy load of catharsis, the event will be judged not as tragic opera, but as hubristic farce.

CM:
"Miss Sarajevo"

The story may be apocryphal: how Luciano Pavarotti, awakened at dawn by workers renovating the hotel next to his in Portland, went outside in his bathrobe to ask the foreman what it would cost for his crew to take the day off. The foreman made a quick calculation: $25,000. The tenor handed him a wad of hundred-dollar bills and said, *I need my sleep*—which was my first thought early one morning that spring when Serbian artillery in the mountains around Sarajevo began to shell the neighborhood where I was staying. I hurried down to the basement of the house rented to an NGO, and while I took notes on the stories and conversations of different people arriving and departing when there was a lull in the shooting, in another basement in the city Bosnian women competed in the Miss Besieged Sarajevo contest, under a banner reading: **DON'T LET THEM KILL US.** This dark humor inspired a documentary film and a song, composed by Bono and Brian Eno, which U2 debuted at Pavarotti's annual benefit concert in his hometown of Modena, Italy. The concert, which he dedicated to the children of Bosnia, was a glitzy affair that drew celebrities like Princess Diana to hear him add a solo to "Miss Sarajevo"—a mournful blend of pop music and opera. The YouTube video of the song, which includes footage of a man sprinting across Sniper Alley, the contestants in bathing suits, and the National Library in flames, has seventeen million views. The winner of the contest, Inela Nogić, who might have been mistaken for Diana's younger sister, lives now in the Netherlands. Not long ago she accused the band of profiting for twenty-five years from that video. *Wouldn't it have been decent to pay us for that?* she asked.

MB:
The Future

The timeworn movie house in our small town showed films only on week-ends. Small-business owners like my father were given tickets to hand out. I no longer remember the gimmick, which might have been that each free ticket required a paid companion, since rarely would anyone go to a movie alone. Movies were for dates and families. Matinees, when the lights went down, someone would throw open the exit door near the front. While the light from the alley washed away the screen, a dozen kids would pour in, scattering into seats so that the usher could find and expel only one or two. Double features were common, along with previews, news, a short subject, a cliff-hanging serial and a cartoon. And there was sometimes more: the annual raf-fle of Thanksgiving turkeys or a talent show, the volume of applause determining the winners. Usually, there was a boyfriend whistling and shout-ing for his favorite. The contestants were solidly amateur in a community characterized by polka combos and singers who could emcee wedding re-ceptions. The just-betrothed honeymooned at places they could drive to: Bear Mountain, Niagara Falls... As they drove away, cardboard signs flap-ping against the trunk and tin cans dragging from the rear bumper, every car honked. How long ago? The only bathing beauty shows were modest films from Atlantic City. No sleazy Trump pageants, nor a twit for a President. Such behavior was inconceivable. The future always is, and here we are. Here & now.

CM:
The Past

Walmart's decision to turn 160 parking lots into drive-in movie theaters, a creative response to the closing of cineplexes during the pandemic, stirred in me nostalgia for the Somerville Drive-In, on Route 22, where I saw *Easy Rider*. An online search yielded the fact that New Jersey was home to the first drive-in, which opened in June 1933—three months after Hitler used the Reichstag fire to consolidate power; the last one closed in 1991. A miniature golf course, with a heated driving range and two indoor golf simulators, stands on the site of the Somerville Drive-In, one of more than 20,000 movie theaters demolished around the world. It is only a fifteen-minute drive to the Trump National Golf Club in Bedminster, where the Hall of Fame quarterback Brett Favre joined the president for a round today, while the American death toll from the coronavirus approached 150,000 and paramilitary forces clashed with Black Lives Matter protesters on the streets of Portland, Oregon. On Mardi Gras, in a French Quarter cemetery, Dennis Hopper and Peter Fonda drop acid with two prostitutes, played by Toni Basil and Karen Black; their bad trip is the prelude to the violent climax of the film, when a redneck shoots both men off their motorcycles—a scene that shocked my stoned friends and me at the drive-in. Trump is a notorious cheater at golf, and Favre's memory loss from the concussions he suffered on the football field may prevent him from remembering that he was once accused of sexting the game-day host for the New York Jets. How many mulligans are permitted in the authoritarian's playbook?

MB:
Ready, Aim, Focus

It must have been our ages then that so deeply embedded feelings rooted in the drive-in movies of the Fifties. Before selling our Northwest retreat in 2019, we made a point to go to a show at the Wheel-In-Motor drive-in. Families lugging folding chairs and picnic baskets. No longer the technical gee-whiz of what was once the Date Night Passion Pit from which movie-goers accidentally ripped the small speakers from their posts as they drove away. No longer the monstrous illusion that powered Peter Bogdanovich's 1968 crime thriller, *Targets*, in which an aging yet still imposing Boris Karloff frightens a sniper shooting from behind the massive screen. Bogdanovich's film paralleled Charles Whitman's 1966 shootings from atop the University of Texas-Austin Tower that today boasts seven lighting configurations. What will be the title of the horror film in which Donald Trump sends tens of thousands of Americans to their graves for the sake of the stock market? *The Republican Party of Death? To Die for the Dow?* Trump would hate *Come Back to the Five and Dime, Jimmy Dean, Jimmy Dean*, in which Karen Black, in perhaps her best role, plays the character Joe who has become Joanne. The prospect of Trump having a heart, courage or a brain suggests, not *The Wizard of Oz*, but *Mission Impossible*.

CM:
Open Secrets

Impossible to divine what led my college soccer teammate to take his life—
this was the verdict of our coach and classmates. I had not seen him since
graduation, but I could not resist the temptation to speculate about his deci-
sion in political terms, if only because my disdain for his success as an in-
vestment banker and Republican operative was colored by jealousy. I dated
his former girlfriend, briefly, near the end of my internship at the Freedom
to Write Committee in New York, mindful that my passion for Polish poets
and the Solidarity movement was nothing compared to what she had felt
with him at Reagan's inauguration ball, and when we separated I locked them
both away in a vault in my mind marked *Privileged*. She married another class-
mate, he took a job at Treasury, and OpenSecrets.org kept track of his do-
nations to Republican politicians amounting to more than half a million
dollars. Did he lose heart over his party's failure to contain the pandemic or
salvage the economy? It was convenient to think so in a summer of social
unrest, disease, and death. NOAA forecasts so many storms this hurricane
season it may have to employ the Greek alphabet to name them all—which
brought to mind what Casca says to Cassius in the first act of *Julius Caesar:*
"But, for mine own part, it was Greek to me." I felt the same about my former
teammate's fate. He was an attacking midfielder, like me, and a canny play-
maker who had a gift for distributing the ball to teammates running into
open spaces. He never seemed to break a sweat. What happened?

MB:
What Happened?

The straight-line winds of the derecho that hit Iowa August 10, 2020, gusted to 140 miles per hour inside rain and hail, tore apart large trees, knocked out cell towers, canceled radio, TV and the Internet, and cut off power that could not be restored to thousands for many days. We were in the basement for an hour and a half while the winds ripped a power line conduit pipe from the side of the house, and broken trees took down electric lines and lay across them like dying Republican elephants. The Democratic virtual convention began one week later. While Trump tweeted hatred and lies, the Democrats promised to undo the dark of the past three years. In the news of the days, it was barely noted that the Senate Intelligence Committee had concluded that Russia had indeed interfered to get Trump elected. I can understand how an ethical Republican might be depressed beyond recovery by the likelihood of collusion and treason. The straw that breaks the elephant's back might also be any of Trump's corrupt and inept appointees, from Attorney General Barr to Postmaster General DeJoy. How can a Republican banker look away from Jared Kushner's decision to deep-six a coronavirus testing program because, Kushner realized, the virus was mainly killing Democratic voters? Ignore this or that? Maybe he can't. What happened to our nation's soul? How reclaim it? Notwithstanding the popular song that says otherwise, wishing will not make it so.

CM:
The Periodic Law

Gustavus Hinrichs, the Danish chemist who identified the straight-line storm phenomenon known as the derecho, from the Spanish word for *direct,* possessed what his biographer called an "almost maniacal passion" for teaching at the University of Iowa. He and his wife immigrated at the start of the Civil War, and when she died, six months after Robert E. Lee surrendered his army in the village of Appomattox Court House, he decided to marry her sister. He was an irascible polymath, fluent in five languages, whose research and publications in astronomy, geology, meteorology, and physics were balanced by his feuds with colleagues and university administrators; his Chart of the Elements was a forerunner to the Periodic Table, his labyrinthine approach to classification being superseded by what became the periodic law: *When elements are arranged in order of increasing atomic number, there is a periodic repetition of their chemical and physical properties.* Consider the elements of our body politic, agitated in their different ways in this summer of dread: how the repetition of certain lines of argument can lead to violence; how common it is in conversation to be reminded of the rancor that preceded the Confederate attack on Fort Sumter. Iowa's senior senator has blessed the Trump campaign's use of Russian disinformation, while his constituents clear debris from the derecho, throw out spoiled food, wait for power to be restored. After Hinrichs quit the university in a huff, he moved to St. Louis, where he invented an embalming fluid to sell to morticians. This confirms the wisdom of a quote mistakenly attributed to Mark Twain—*History never repeats itself but it rhymes.* There is a straight line from the Civil War to American Carnage.

MB:
Champagne at Madame Quartz's in Tangier

If the Internet were to be trusted, many of the most popular and amusing aphoristic sayings belong to Mark Twain, Oscar Wilde or Yogi Berra, who said only some of what they are said to have said. Political figures don't need to say anything to be quoted. British writer Nigel Rees called misattributions to Winston Churchill "Churchillian Drift." So: does it matter that Einstein didn't say it or Freud didn't say it? Anonymity is the new byline, but celebrity is validation. Today, August 29, 2020, aphorisms about government seem reversible. Is it that those who do not know history are doomed to repeat it, or that those who know history are doomed to repeat it? Now, when fascism has taken up residence in the White House, I can better stomach a quip from other quarters. In the sports world, coach John Wooden told his basketball teams, "Be quick but don't hurry." The distinction is brilliant. For philosophy and the limits of language, the Jewish aphorism, "If you can't get up, get down; if you can't get across, get across." Fleeing the news (getting across?), I was driven to making mental lists of small pleasures. Backlot at the circus, seeing the elephants pull up the tent poles. Standing in the movie star's bathtub for a photo. One particular pass I made as a young basketball player. Learning that in Judaism study is equivalent to prayer. Shave ice in Hawai'i, ice cream custard on the dock in Howth, Vietnamese coffee near the Sydney Opera House, profiteroles in Connemara. Lunch at Georges atop the Pompidou. I recollect dinners at Pasha in Prague, Christina's on Orcas Island, The Black Locust in Fish Creek, Natalia's in Macon. Until the day we cure the body politic of COVID-19 and the malady that is Trump, such sensory memories are a salve.

CM:
The Tomb of Ibn Battuta

To What Do I Belong? was the title of a summit I hosted in Tangier, a mythical city in the literary imagination and the birthplace of the great traveler, Ibn Battuta, a medieval jurist (with whom I share a birthday) who spent thirty years visiting every country in the disintegrating empire of Islam and beyond. He racked up 75,000 miles in transit, by land and sea, to Cairo and Mecca, Central Asia and Siberia, India and China, never following the same trade or pilgrim route twice. He interviewed sheiks and saints; survived shipwrecks, pirate attacks, uprisings; married often; when the Sultan recalled him to Morocco, he dictated an entertaining account of his travels, which has furnished historians with a vision of 14th-century Islamic society and inspired my own cultural diplomacy missions. I hoped his spirit of adventure would animate my discussions with ten writers from around the world. Traversing and bridging differences was our theme, and we met in the American Legation Museum, a Moorish-style building in the medina that marks the origins of American diplomacy, invoking writers who had lived or visited here: Paul Bowles, George Orwell, Jean Genet, and Mark Twain, who wrote, "Tangier is the spot we have been longing for all the time." A Russian novelist from Dagestan observed that when she moved to Moscow the different strands of her ethnic makeup—Avar, Iranian, Jewish, Central Asian princes—led the security services to bring her in regularly for questioning. Her Avar tongue-twisters charmed us all. She wrote: "Step by step, I cast aside my identities and came to the conclusion that any belonging is divisive." Perhaps Ibn Battuta's travels led him to a similar conclusion. When we entered his tomb on a tour of the port city, I recalled his saying: *Traveling—it leaves you speechless, then turns you into a storyteller.* My thirty years on the road came to a sudden end in the pandemic: what stories would I tell about that woman who left me speechless?

MB:
Expats

I was eager to feel part of each expatriate community I encountered—Mexico, Spain, Tangier—but each time it proved beyond my sensibility to so adapt. Not even to adapt, but just to feel I could be a member. But no, I remained an expat community of one. In Mexico, I had money, young and half-employed as I was, with which to pay a cook, a cleaner, a laundress and the groundskeeper. They depended on me, and indeed it took some rudimentary sleight of hand to tip them extra for whatever reason without incurring the wrath of the expats happy to be minimal. In Spain, where my acquaintances shifted fluidly from Spanish to French to English and back, I was the kid from only one country. In Tangier, I felt only mildly engrossed by a stoned Paul Bowles' good nature and the erotic narratives of his boy storyteller. It felt to me that it was always just about time to go. Never to arrive, but to somehow have found oneself somewhere at the moment when it was time to go. I laugh to contrast this with my total comfort in New York City cabs where the drivers speak but a little jumbled American. I like checking their names and countries of origin on the backs of the front seats. My favorite city hacks? The driver named Purchase Slaughter, who wheeled me around Chicago. And the Nigerian who took me by way of a D.C. storefront at midnight where his cabbie countrymen needed to do some late night business. And yes, I agreed. I am of immigrant stock, but not of expat stock. They came to stay. And to meld. And to assimilate. Not to stay apart in expat land. Not to think of themselves as emotionally elsewhere. Not that. I remain more a part of Tombstone City than of Paris. I admit it. Of course I like Paris, Prague, Marfil in Mexico, Nerja in Spain, and the many others. It was always best as an outsider.

CM:
Cognac

In the first winter of the war, a military monitor arranged for me to interview the Yugoslav Army general who had orchestrated the siege of Dubrovnik; when Croatian authorities barred me from crossing the border into Montenegro, I took a bus from that medieval city to Split, caught a flight to Zagreb, and boarded a train to Budapest, intending to travel to Belgrade and Podgorica, where the general was stationed. This added nearly 1,700 kilometers to my itinerary. Not far from the Hungarian border, I developed an acute pain in my ankle, around the scar from the surgical removal of a ganglion cyst some years before, and decided to seek treatment in Budapest. I could walk and run, but sleep evaded me in my rented room until I draped my leg over the side of the bed. In the morning, the elderly landlady ordered me to drink a shot of cognac before I left to search, in vain, for a doctor—our daily ritual until I departed for Serbia. The pain vanished as mysteriously as it arose, and by the time I met the general, more than a week later, in the officer's club at his base, I was prepared for anything—except the monotony of the typewritten answers to the questions I had faxed him in advance, which he insisted on reading aloud. His translators and orderlies seemed to relish my discomfort in the face of his patent falsehoods, and while I knew it could be dangerous to interrupt him—I was, after all, a freelance journalist—I asked him why he had allowed his troops to commit so many atrocities. Nothing rattled him. Nor did he reply. But I was becoming more adept at ferreting out the truth from the dark arts of propaganda. A waiter arrived to serve us slivovitz. *Živeli,* I said when we clinked glasses. Long life.

MB:
Scotch

You would have had to have been there to see with what gusto we threw our-
selves into our adolescence. Teen boys in the Puritan Fifties, we formed a
stag party each New Year's Eve. The ultimate plan was to crash a coed party
just before midnight in the hope that some pretty girl might kiss us. First,
we shaped a pyramid of bottles of booze and laid in a multitude of cookies
and chips as well as ill-advised sausages. Roger showed up with his cornet
case, shaking it to show how he had snuck the liquor out of his house. I al-
ways brought bourbon. We hung streamers. Then we took a photo of the
booze pyramid before embarking on a sea of drink and acting as silly as
good friends can be in adolescence. Indeed, it was The Night of Our Ad-
olescence by which all successive juvenile behavior in the new year was to be
judged. This night, someone had rigged fireworks to my Plymouth, so that
when I tried to sneak out a little early to find a kiss that might not be avail-
able after midnight, a quick burst of fireworks gave me away. Then on we
went, arriving at the party where our booze-strengthened nerve and good
timing would surely win us the unending passion of, say, three seconds. I
went to the kitchen for one last bracer, bypassing other forms of alcohol to
swill some scotch, after which I threw up. I have never been able to take a
taste of scotch since. No kisses. How is taste made? From taste buds on the
tongue, of which a fussy eater is now known to have more? From expectation?
From associations with a hope of romance? The song that filled the airwaves
was, "What Are You Doing New Year's Eve?" Me, I was throwing up. Years
later, I always brought ouzo to parties. Turn a seemingly empty ouzo bottle
upside down, and you can usually get three more drops. I drank ouzo in Tan-
gier, slivovitz in Serbia, Guinness every day in Ireland, and Victoria Bitter in
Sydney. I have a taste for other lands and a diffidence toward New Year's
Eve.

CM:
Ouzo

My first taste of ouzo came on the day my grandmother and I finished packing her belongings for her move to a condominium. She was a Christian Scientist afflicted with tic douloureux, and she liked to listen to taped lectures about the mind's healing properties, with clothespins affixed to her fingers to distract her from what one doctor called *an exquisitely agonizing facial pain syndrome*; when she left for church that morning, I hiked through the neighbor's dairy farm and adjoining woods to Ledell's Pond, where in my last year of high school I had skated every morning before class, and followed a dirt road to a wooded hillside on another neighbor's property—the halfway point in a six-mile loop I knew like the back of my hand. Uphill I walked until I met an old family friend, Pony Wood, who was clearing brush. He pointed at a *No Trespassing* sign posted on a tree, demanding to know my name—which he did not recognize. When I told him I was staying at my grandmother's house, which he had visited regularly over many decades, he professed not to know who she was. Had he lost his mind? I wondered when he ordered me to leave his land. I headed for Tempe Wick Road, where I failed to hitch a ride home; by the time I returned, my grandmother was not only riddled with anxiety but in great pain. On the kitchen table she set out a bottle of ouzo, which she had brought back from a trip to Greece, and insisted we drink to a future rich in travel to foreign lands—which at that time was impossible for me to imagine. Yet one day I found myself sipping ouzo with a monk on the Holy Mountain of Athos, in northern Greece, where in the fourteenth century these anise-flavored spirits were first distilled. If the monk believed I had no business being there, he kept that to himself, and on my departure for the mainland he gave me an icon of Saint Nicholas the Wonderworker, the patron saint of sailors, merchants, children, prostitutes, pawnbrokers, students, and repentant thieves.

MB:
Versions

The south shore of Long Island afforded woods with enough space between trees that one could build a flimsy fort. The Pine Barrens were a ways down the highway, so we conjured a thicker arboreal life in uncut backyards and sea-life at decrepit docks. Plenty of beaches but few woods where the Island, as it forked east toward Montauk and Orient Points, was increasingly too porous for roots. A drive upstate to thicker woods was an event. Are we not versions of one another? Your six-mile walking loop is my biking to the Coast Guard Station. Your ice skating before class is my handball off the windowless brick wall of the school building. It is true that location is destiny. Think famine and flood, war and peace, malaria and Ebola. Then give a nod to the smaller influences: woods or water, sunstroke or frostbite. We are the sum of too much ever to be delineated. "...a future rich in travel to foreign lands" meant The Big Apple and, someday, Florida. Your sipping ouzo with a monk at a holy site is my drinking hot chocolate late at night with the Dean who has taken me, in my role as newspaper editor to the site of a faculty suicide. Your mastery of gardening is my occasional work on a duck farm. In Port Townsend, our cross-street neighbor Lou cut down any tree that tried his yard. He didn't want the crows, the leaves, or the effect of storms off the cliff at road's end, whereas we let stand large trees that overtook our personal water view with dense foliage. Could *"higgledy-piggledy"* be a true characterization of a life, and Popeye's the last word: "I yam what I yam"?

CM:
Reduplication

Like you, I did not speak as a toddler until a complete sentence formed on my tongue. *My Daddy has gone to work,* I said one morning just before my second birthday, relieving my mother of her fear that my silence signaled a debilitating mental condition, in the same way that in my infancy a military doctor's decision to snip the band of tissue connecting my tongue to the floor of my mouth absolved her of blame for the malnourishment I suffered in my first months of life before anyone figured out that I was getting no milk from breastfeeding. If we are versions of one another, then perhaps our early silence was a form of waiting for syntax—which is what poets in every language share between writing one poem and the next. When my older daughter, Hannah, was little, she pronounced Pinocchio in a sing-song fashion, *No . . . no,* eliding the syllables she could not wrap her tongue around—which led me to conclude that rhythm is essential not only to the acquisition of language and the arts of poetry, music, and dance, but to everything we care about. Hannah loved Pinocchio, and I loved how her face lit up when she said, *No . . . no*—a rhyming compound, in linguistic terms, or reduplication, like *higgledy-piggledy* or *hocus-pocus.* Any sound can spark memory or imagination, and as we wait for the votes to be counted in what the pundits are calling the most important election of our lifetime, I savor the sound and taste of certain words: Montauk, Orient Point, Erie Lackawanna—the train that took me to Hoboken, and then the world.

MB:
All Aboard

Sept. 9, 1969. New York Governor Nelson Rockefeller says the Long Island Railroad will be the best commuter line in the nation by October 7 or "I won't be around." The L.I.R.R. is facing a revolt, riders refusing to pay for the filthy cars of locked windows in which they start and end their workdays in Manhattan. Rockefeller shuts down the line, the cars get washed, and the line is declared the best in the country. A little white lie that rockets through town after town, strap hangers filling the aisles going west to work in the city, those early boarders heading east trying to hog a seat for their shopping. Before the railroad shuttered station after station the length of the island, the lilt of the conductor as he called out the stations ahead was the best part of the ride. The snap of his ticket puncher felt like a confirmation of one's place in the world. The hiss from underneath as one descended on arrival had the effect of a wide broom cleaning up behind you. Driving parallel to the train, one could sometimes blow the horn to elicit a whistle from the engineer. The caboose, off-limits to passengers, was thought to be a homey room where conductors could steady their legs. Nothing aerodynamic about it, the engine labored to punch holes in inertia before it lumbered forward on the trip to cruising speed. It was a world of distinctive rhythms. Choo-choo, chug and chuff. The squeal on the curves erased for a moment the rhythm of the wheels. In politics, too, it's a rhythm if it lets you breathe, it's a drone if it stops up your ears.

CM:
Mending Hill

I must have been seven when my mother put me on a train one summer morning to visit her parents in Maryland. There were more toys than clothes in my suitcase, and the shoebox I brought aboard contained dried grass and a litter of newborn rabbits, whose eyes had not opened. Molly, our docile English springer spaniel, had surprised us when she pounced on a rabbit emerging from its burrow and wrung its neck until it went limp. I was certain that feeding the hairless kits warm milk with an eyedropper would ensure their survival, and the conductor humored me until he was replaced in Philadelphia by a young man, who dismissed my efforts with a wave of his ticket puncher; also my tears when two kits died before I got out in Baltimore. My grandparents indulged my quixotic undertaking on the drive to their house, which doubled as a doctor's office named *Mending Hill*. But after dinner, when my grandfather went downstairs to see patients, my grandmother told me the remaining kits would not last the night. For the rest of my stay I memorized batting averages in the newspaper, fished the creek, left pennies on the railroad tracks for a train that never seemed to arrive. Brooks Robinson was on his way to winning the MVP when the Civil Rights Act was signed into law, and I was home before LBJ used the Gulf of Tonkin incident to justify the war in Vietnam—two facts I did not connect until I read your Choo-choo, chug and chuff.

MB:
Light at the End of the Tunnel

I have a habit of first saying "logarithmic" when I mean "exponential." I suppose it's an unconscious wish for a time when there were noticeable intervals between newsworthy events. My college fiction writing teacher explained fiction with the example of a man boarding a train. By the end of the trip something will have changed. The murder will have been solved on the Orient Express, the prisoners will make it to Switzerland... In a time of noticeable intervals, there was time still for nostalgia. Trains and train stations could be important to the plot. Remember when meet-ups were scheduled to take place under the big clock at Grand Central Station? You knew something was coming if you waited for it. At the movies, if Tom Mix fell from a cliff, you knew a week's wait would give you an answer to what happened. I have a friend who starts a book by reading the ending. She wants to know ahead of time how she'll feel afterward. The word "logarithm" was coined by Scottish mathematician John Napier in the 1600s from the Greek words *logos* and *arithmos*, which together make "ratio-number." Logarithmic growth being the inverse of exponential growth, I can perhaps be forgiven for my tendency to say logarithmic first. It's safer. It offers the hope that we will not be run over by an exponential rise in population, right-wing rancor or climate catastrophes. Once one had time to breathe between changes that affected us. Superstition had a role. Don't step on a sidewalk crack or break a mirror. Step over the baseline chalk when running on or off the field. Knock on wood. Actions inserted into the predictable. In the Age of the Exponential, we have to squint to spot the intervals. November 14, 2020. Everyday-something-Trump is an exponential continuum of lies. Where are the intervals? Where is the station? When did this train ride become a runaway? Tunnel after tunnel was fun once. Not now.

CM:
Intervals

As in the relationship in pitch between two different notes. Or the running regimen I followed as a college soccer player in the off-season. Or the time I spent on transoceanic flights before the pandemic. Once, flying from LAX to Maui, I upgraded to first class with miles collected from my Balkan travels, and passed several delightful hours in the company of an actress whose recent divorce from her more famous actor-husband had effectively ended not only her career but her contact with celebrities she had imagined to be her friends. Liam Neeson's name came up, and she explained his smile at the Academy Awards ceremony, when he did not win Best Actor for his role as Oskar Schindler, as a Hollywood ritual: he would be rewarded one day for not betraying his true feelings. *Short Cuts* was available on in-flight entertainment, and as we compared notes on its fidelity to the original Raymond Carver stories I wondered if she had feelings for me. Time flew by. Just before landing I said that between reporting trips to Sarajevo I liked to stopover in Zurich to sit in a pew at the Fraumünster, gazing at Marc Chagall's stained-glass windows. I found solace in his biblical scenes, which he regarded as "a transparent partition between my heart and the heart of the world." I should have asked her for her number. This is what haunts me in the interval between Joe Biden's election and his inauguration, even as I try to differentiate between the traitorous notes that Trump and his supporters are sounding—*Rigged election! Fraud!*—and the ordinary music of a functioning democracy. I wish I had her number.

MB:
Shy

I admire the facility with which you talk easily with the famous and accomplished. Upon meeting me for the first time, my mother-in-law said to Dorothy, "He's shy." Later, I would be gregarious among an international cast of military people for whom I arranged visits to museums, factories and a world's fair. I spoke easily to visiting generals because there wasn't much to say. I always felt at home conversationally among workers and sales clerks. Among the famous, however, I clammed up. Exiting the elevator into a Manhattan apartment to spot Abba Eban talking with Barbara Walters, and elsewhere in the room Andy Warhol, George Plimpton and others of like stature, I headed for the kitchen to sit silently with a drunken Tennessee Williams. Taken to a party at Mark Rothko's I spoke to no one. I have been remembering the deep silence of the Rothko chapel in Houston where I sat among his framed color-fields, unable to put aside the fact of his suicide; hence, unable to converse with the paintings. I come from a town where there was neither satire nor irony. You could call our talk blunt. It took up the times and the occasions without nuance or even asides. Given the way it was, I grew silent. What began as shyness became refusal. I became a counter puncher. The other person had to start. I would like to believe that Rothko's color-fields added to his life, that they are not essentially lonely and despondent. Writing to the *New York Times*, he said, "We are for the large shape because it has the impact of the unequivocal." He recommended that viewers stand as little as eighteen inches from his large canvases so as to experience intimacy and the unknown. Sitting in the Rothko chapel, I thought the artist's color-fields not shy but wary.

CM:

Untitled (Black on Grey)

What I took from the 1978 Mark Rothko retrospective at the Guggenheim was the steady darkening of his vision: how the restricted palette of his late Color-Field abstractions matched my mood as I followed my college girl-friend up the ramp gallery toward the skylight. S. was an art history major in search of a topic for her thesis, and I was hoping she would not betray me when she went home for Christmas. Frank Lloyd Wright's joke on New York was where I grasped two basic truths: that I would lose S. and that Rothko's words—"The people who weep before my pictures are having the same religious experience I had when I painted them"—would shape my writing life. When S. called on New Year's Eve to say she had met someone, I drank myself into oblivion night after night. It was so cold that winter in Vermont that pipes laid six feet underground burst, and it was twenty below when I set out one morning to pick up S. at the Burlington airport. My car jerked downhill, as if I did not know how use the stick-shift; the emergency brake had frozen, so I left the car at the gas station to thaw and hitchhiked north in my windbreaker, sockless and hungover. S. did not speak on the bus ride back, and I shook uncontrollably. Nevertheless in the spring, when she was unable to begin her thesis, I agreed to write it for her, arguing that the progression of Rothko's work made his suicide inevitable. Thus in *Black on Grey, 1970*, which dates from the last year of his life, I found evidence in the different shades of black atop a grey rectangle that he would soon cut an exit for himself from the tyranny of the blank canvas. S. got a B+ for what I produced in three days—an Easter miracle, I joked, which did not save our relationship. *Tragic experience*, Rothko said, *is the only source book for art.* S. went on to marry my best friend.

MB:

Now

Afterword

"I like to think we have a world right here," Marvin Bell wrote. His was a world predicated on the mystery of the creative process, which he called *Bloody Brainwork* in his last lecture. He had at his command an array of formal strategies, techniques, and gifts, and he was a relentless explorer, who kept pushing past terrain surveyed by others. His concerns—emotional, aesthetic, philosophical, political—were wide-ranging, befitting his restless imagination. He was by turns a prophet and a comic, a singer and a wise man, whose work belongs to the tradition of wisdom literature, which stretches from Ecclesiastes to Emily Dickinson, a tutelary spirit hovering in the background of his poems. He wrote book-length sequences; carried on a poetic dialogue with William Stafford; composed poems in prose. "Writing is all and everything, when you care," he observed in "Instructions to Be Left Behind." What distinguishes his work was the care and attention he devoted not only to the art and craft of writing poetry but to every moment in his life and in the lives of others—which may account for his ability to reimagine himself as a poet at every stage of his career. Thus when it seemed as if he had explored every possible aspect of the free verse lyric he surprised readers with his invention of the Dead Man Poems, which were collected in *Incarnate*. These two-part meditations begin with the Zen admonition, *Live as if you were already dead*, and proceed to examine every side of everything from the perspective of an everyman always conscious that the end is near at hand.

Left unspoken was the understanding that our collaboration, which was to last for nearly ten years, might come to an untimely end. Marvin liked to call the study of poetry a survival skill—something that helped its practitioners live fuller lives. The prose poems or paras, as we liked to call them, that we exchanged were thus a record of two men of different generations—Marvin was twenty years older than me—engaged in a conversation that became central to each of us.

Marvin was born in New York City on 3 August 1937, to a Jewish family of immigrants from Ukraine, raised in Center Moriches, Long Island, and served as a lieutenant in the U.S. Army. He earned a bachelor's degree from Alfred University, a master's degree from the University of Chicago, and an MFA from the Iowa Writers' Workshop, where he taught for forty years, retiring as the Flannery O'Connor Professor of Letters; his students are a Who's Who of American poetry. He held Senior Fulbright appointments to Yugoslavia and Australia and was Iowa's first Poet Laureate. "I'll tell you right now the secrets of writing poetry," he once said. "First, one learns to write by reading. ... Number two, I believe that language, compared to the materials of other art forms, has only one thing going for it: the ability to be precise. ... And the third and most important secret is that, if you do anything seriously for a long time, you get better at it." Marvin's poetry offers abundant proof of this insight. He wrote well until his final days.

Determined to find clarifying words for what remains invisible to others, Marvin translated his individual experiences into poems that double as life lessons, and passed along to several generations of students what he learned from his immersion in poetry from many lands. He placed a high value on listening closely to other poets, within the classroom and without; the exercises in imitation he assigned, which he did himself, were designed to tune the ear to other possibilities, which in his work was transformed into something new, as in his "Poem After Carlos Drummond de Andrade" or the three poems he wrote, on assignment, on the subject of ecstasy—this from a man who claimed to "hold to/ a certain sadness the way others/ search for joy, though I like joy." What he praised as a poet's ability to listen to his materials, to meditate on the potential music and meaning of every word, image, and idea, is on lavish display in all his books.

His shaping influence on my life dates from the summer of 1978, when I studied with him at the Bread Loaf Writers' Conference; his poems, essays, and interviews would school me in the art and craft of poetry, the intricacies of the creative process, and the nature of artistic camaraderie. Our friendship began in earnest some years later, when he took a sabbatical leave in Santa Fe, New Mexico, where my wife and I were caretakers of an estate on the edge of the national forest. Marvin called me nearly every morning to talk, gossip, joke, and banter—calls I came to regard as invaluable life lessons. Poetry begins with listening, and I was grateful for the chance to listen to him. A seed was planted in those conversations for what grew into a fruitful collaboration.

Ours was inspired by his earlier partnership with Stafford, which produced a magnetic book titled *Segues*, and a fine-press edition, *Annie-Over*. Stafford wrote: "Marvin Bell is easy to interchange with. Like a prism, he accepts whatever comes at him and reflects it in rainbows." This was my experience, too, first in the group poem collaboration we undertook in 2007 to celebrate the International Writing Program's fortieth anniversary, *7 Poets, 4 Days, 1 Book*, and then in the exchange of prose poems collected in *After the Fact*, the first volume of which, *Scripts & Postscripts*, was published in 2016. From the beginning we probed our memories, teased out the meaning of various public and private events, bore witness to our separate walks in the sun. Nothing excited me more in literary terms than this exploration. Marvin seemed to feel the same. "I love receiving each new para from you," he wrote upon receiving in early December 2020 what turned out to be my, and our, last installment in *Here & Now*. "It defines the immediate future." Some hours later, he sent me a final message: "Heartbreaking." His family was with him when he died a few days later, and the stereo was playing Chet Baker's "You'd Be So Nice To Come Home To."

Marvin never missed a beat.

About the Authors

Marvin Bell was the author of more than twenty books of poetry, including *Mars Being Red, Rampant, Iris of Creation,* and *Drawn by Stones, by Earth, by Things That Have Been in the Fire.* His works included collaborations with musicians, composers, dancers, poets and photographers—among them, poet William Stafford and photographer Nathan Lyons—and volumes of an original poetic form collected in *Incarnate: The Collected Dead Man Poems.* Among his literary honors were awards from the Academy of American Poets, the American Academy of Arts and Letters, the Guggenheim Foundation, the National Endowment for the Arts, and *The American Poetry Review.* He was the Flannery O'Connor Professor of Letters at the Iowa Writers' Workshop, where he taught for forty years, Iowa's first Poet Laureate, and a professor in the brief-residency MFA program located in Oregon at Pacific University. He lived in Iowa City, Iowa, and Port Townsend, Washington, until his death on December 14, 2020.

Christopher Merrill has published eight collections of poetry, including *Watch Fire,* for which he received the Lavan Younger Poets Award from the Academy of American Poets; many edited volumes and translations; and six books of nonfiction, among them, *Only the Nails Remain: Scenes from the Balkan Wars, Things of the Hidden God: Journey to the Holy Mountain,* and *Self-Portrait with Dogwood.* His writings have been translated into nearly forty languages; his journalism appears widely; his honors include a Chevalier des Arts et des Lettres from the French government, numerous translation awards, and fellowships from the John Simon Guggenheim Memorial and Ingram Merrill Foundations. As director of the International Writing Program at the University of Iowa since 2000, Merrill has conducted cultural diplomacy missions to more than fifty countries. He served on the U.S. National Commission for UNESCO from 2011-2018; in April 2012, President Barack Obama appointed him to the National Council on the Humanities.